Developing Creative Thinking to Improve Academic Writing

PART ONE

INTERMEDIATE LEVEL

AZZA ABUGHARSA, PH. D.

ISBN
978-1-5437-4457-6 (sc)
978-1-5437-4458-3 (e)

Print information available on the last page.

To order additional copies of this book, contact
Toll Free 800 101 2657 (Singapore)
Toll Free 1 800 81 7340 (Malaysia)
www.partridgepublishing.com/singapore
orders.singapore@partridgepublishing.com

02/16/2018

PARTRIDGE

To my two mothers

Amna Omar Ben Hameda

and

Misrata

Preface

Developing Creative Thinking to Improve Academic Writing, Part One is the first of two-part book series that is mainly addressed to international students at intermediate level of English proficiency, though students who are native speakers of English can also benefit from it. This book is helpful for college students as well as students in adult school programs in which different academic writing tasks are required. The purpose of this book is to motivate students to think critically and analyze the topic in hand from multiple perspectives. Accordingly, the book offers a creative approach to help students develop creative thinking required to tackle common topics from uncommon perceptions in order to generate new ideas to make the students more creative, confident and independent in their writing.

Chapter Review

The book chapters are organized in an order that starts from writing a short paragraph to writing compare and contrast essays. The chapters also include working on different kinds of thesis statements as well as details to practice linking all the information provided to the main idea of the topic.

Chapter one is an introductory discussion to write a short paragraph. It presents an explanation of the writing format with examples. Moreover, it discusses how to generate a topic sentence and how to derive different ideas for one topic, and connect the ideas with transition words to join them in one sentence and link two subsequent paragraphs. Lastly, chapter one includes a discussion about paraphrasing sentences and provides different examples and exercises about rephrasing sentences and maintaining their meanings.

In chapter two, the discussion focuses on writing an outline and building a short paragraph starting from the brainstorming step followed by the outline step. After that, the chapter provides a practice of forming the three paragraph components; the introduction, the body, and the conclusion. Discussion on forming the thesis statement is also included with explanation of the difference between general vs. specific thesis statement. In addition, developing critical thinking is practiced to generate unfamiliar controlling ideas for commonly used topics in creative writing exercises. The exercises at the end of this chapter motivate students to practice writing about familiar topics from new perspectives in order to develop the ability to analyze the topic from as many different standpoints as possible.

More practice on extending information in the supporting sentences is provided in chapter three to teach the students how to elaborate on the details in a way that expands the writing and maintains the main idea at the same time. This chapter provides a practice on extending a single paragraph into a longer essay by using key words such as adjectives and adverbs to provide more sentences that explain the qualities described by the adjectives and the actions of the verbs. This practice helps the students think creatively and produce new ideas that are connected to the thesis. As a result, students develop the ability to have an argument to which they can provide details to support and be ready to discuss; this skill is specifically beneficial when defending college graduation papers.

Chapter four presents explanation of the important skill of summarizing. After practicing expanding more ideas to the supporting sentences in chapter three, chapter four gives practical strategies to summarize paragraphs and essays by focusing on the main ideas and the key supporting ones. College students, both native and non-native speakers of English need to improve their summarizing skills to write their research proposals, research abstracts and annotated bibliographies. Interestingly, improving the skill of summarizing helps improving reading sub-skills such as skimming and scanning because the students become able to spot the main points in the text, and therefore understand the general meaning of the reading.

The focus of chapter five is on writing compare and contrast essays about different topics such as two objects and two people. Also, practice is provided about comparing and contrasting a novel and a different movie, and a novel and the movie that is based on that novel. The objective of such activities is to develop the students' ability to think critically about the possible relationships that hold between two items that have similarities and differences. Furthermore, transition words to connect sentences in compare and contrast essays are discussed along with steps to writing these essays. For example, the two kinds of outline are explained in this chapter; the block outline and the point-by-point outline. Students practice witting compare and contrast essays in these two styles and can have a personal preference between them.

Exercises are provided at the end of each chapter to motivate the students to test their understanding of the chapter and put it into real practice. Also, the book includes authentic stories about many individuals and photos of them in order to connect writing exercises to the real world and encourage the students to write about personal experiences. Moreover, different quotes are given at the beginning of each chapter to connect it with real-life ideas and perceptions. These quotes are typed in sketches made by the author of the book to provide illustrated descriptions of the meanings of these quotes as an example of conveying the understood message into a sketch.

Suggestions to the Teacher

This book helps teachers develop teaching strategies that encourage creating new ways of thinking to build a philosophy. The teachers can use the examples provided in each chapter to promote class activities either in the form of single, pair, or group work. Furthermore, the exercises at the end of each chapter offer good practice to writing outlines and building paragraphs. In addition, collaborative learning can be applied by assigning one thesis detail to each group of learners to construct a paragraph and connect it to another paragraph that is written by another group. Such a practice helps the students learn paragraph organization strategies and motivates them to use conjunctions and transition words to maintain the sequence of the ideas. Generally speaking, the exercises in this book involve the students in a learning process that develops their ability to solitary work required for academic writing.

To the Students

Developing Creative Thinking to Improve Academic Writing, Part One is an excellent source for college students and students in other adult programs that assign academic writing. Students in academic programs are expected to perform a number of tasks that include but are not limited to writing reviews, proposals, summaries, abstracts, etc. Moreover, students need to practice developing an argument and supporting it with reliable evidence by using academic style of writing that excludes making absolute judgments and emphasizes the likelihood of changing statements once new evidence(s) emerges. In other words, students need to learn how to build an argument by using general phrases, support this argument and be prepared to modify it based on new collected data. The students can use the writing strategies provided in this book to write their class papers which can be qualified as publishable material during their academic careers as well as upon their graduation.

TABLE OF CONTENTS

LIST OF TABLES

LIST OF FIGURES

LIST OF PICTURES

LIST OF DIAGRAMS

Chapter One

Writing Format

"Thinking is like loving and dying; each of us
must do it for himself"

Josiah Royce

Writing in English undergoes a format that is used for any kind of writing. The major three components of this format are *the introduction*, *the body*, and *the conclusion*. These components can be single sentences in case of a short paragraph, or paragraphs as in essays, or even whole chapters as in books. Figure (1) shows the format in writing in English.

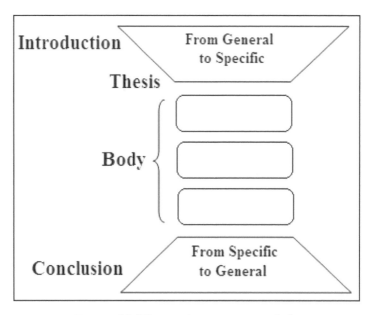

Figure (1) Writing Format in English

As figure (1) shows, the introduction and the conclusion are very similar. In the introductory part, the discussion goes from general to specific. The most specific part is the one that has the main idea (the thesis). For example, if your topic is about the disadvantages of living in your city, you start the introduction by making a general statement that living in big cities has many drawbacks. After that, you narrow the discussion to the specific number of the disadvantages that your city has based on your own opinion. For example:

Living in a big city, despite the many benefits it provides, is full of difficulties and obstacles that can be demanding and stressful. People living in big cities have to deal with the disadvantages in order to find stability and adjustment as they enjoy the opportunities that these cities give. Being a resident of a big city, I have to find a way to put up with disadvantages such as sound pollution, rush hour traffic and high rent.

When writing a conclusion to this topic, the discussion is reversed. In other words, the conclusion starts with a sentence that sums up the disadvantages of living in this city in particular, and then is wrapped up by addressing the challenges of living in big cities in general. Here is an example of such a conclusion:

It is not easy to be surrounded by constant loud noises, heavy traffic and expensive rent. Choosing to live in a big city because of the opportunities it provides entails handling the other negative side of it; it is one package that comes as a whole. As a result, I have to seek a way to adjust in order to deal with these obstacles among other difficulties that large cities are well-known of in order to maintain a good and healthy life styles required to live in metropolitan areas.

The body paragraphs include explanation of details provided in the thesis. Although there is no specific number to these paragraphs, they are generally three or more, depending on the number of details in the thesis required to be covered. As seen, we have chosen three major disadvantages to live in a big city (e.g. sound pollution, high traffic, and expensive rent). We can write at least one sentence for each one of them to construct the body section in a single paragraph, or the body paragraphs in a longer writing.

The body sentences of the paragraph need to be connected with transition words and/ or phrases. This connection is required in all kinds of writing. For example, when writing a short paragraph, transition words are used to connect sentences. In books, the concluding paragraph of each chapter includes sentences that introduce the next chapter, etc. More discussion of transition words is provided later in the chapter.

1.1. Writing Format: The Sandwich

Based on the discussion above, it can be understood that any writing in English must include an introduction, a body, and a conclusion. If the teacher assigns their students a certain topic to write about, every student writes about the topic from their own perspective. As a result, the students have different supporting sentences from one another as each student writes about the topic based on their own background knowledge of it.

For example, if the topic is about the advantages of the graduate program in a certain university, each student talks about a number of advantages that could be different from the advantages another student chooses. However, every essay has an introduction, a body, and a conclusion. And although the introduction and the conclusion are similar in all the essays, the body paragraphs are not the same regardless of their relevance to the main idea.

This is similar to a sandwich (picture 1) which has a piece of bread on top (introduction/ topic sentence), a piece of bread on the bottom (conclusion/ concluding sentence) and some other elements in between such as lettuce, tomato slices, cheese, etc (body/ supporting sentences). Like a sandwich, the difference is in the elements inside. For example, one person chooses not to have onions in their sandwich, another person has only lettuce and cheese, and yet a third person wants tomatoes only. Nevertheless, they all have some elements between the two pieces of bread. This is the case in writing.

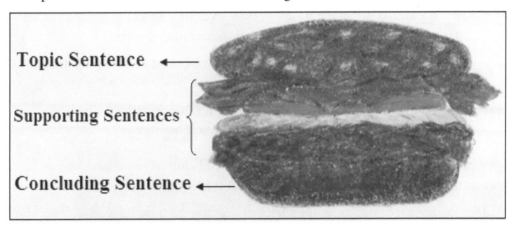

Picture 1, Writing Format in English

Let's practice organizing topic details in accordance to the three items of the sandwich. The topic is about the reporter Fouad who has other plans for his career.

Reporter Fouad at work

Ideas (brainstorming): Fouad originally wants to be a successful soccer player. However, this does not work out so he decides to work in the media. He becomes a successful reporter.

Here is an example of how to classify this information about Fouad into an introduction, a body, and a conclusion based on the sandwich format:

Introduction (top bread): Great achievements require commitment and determination.

Thesis: Fouad works hard because he wants to be successful and well-known in his career.

Body (ingredients): Fouad first starts by practicing soccer. Things do not work out as he desires, so he decided to work in the media instead.

Conclusion (bottom bread): Fouad becomes a famous reporter because he is a hard-working determined individual.

This is more illustrated in picture 2

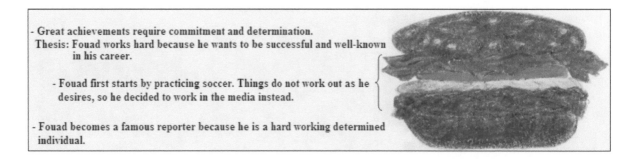

Picture 2, elements of a paragraph about reporter Fouad

Each section can be formed based on the type of writing. For example, if you are writing a short paragraph, then the introduction and conclusion can be one sentence each, and the body section usually contains from three to five sentences.

This is not very different in case of writing an essay. One paragraph can be assigned to the introduction and another paragraph to the conclusion. The introduction starts with a general statement about succeeding through hard work. The paragraph ends up with the thesis statement about how Fouad achieves success by being very determined.

As for the body paragraphs, their number depends on the details under discussion. We understand that Fouad's major goal is to become successful, and that his initial desire is to become a soccer player. These two pieces of information can be included in one body paragraph, with some sentences constructed to give the reason(s) why Fouad cannot pursue his soccer career. In the second body paragraph, the discussion focuses on the shift from soccer to media. The sentences are about the reason(s) that makes Fouad choose media for his career. Also, this paragraph gives information about how Fouad becomes a successful reporter.

Finally, the concluding paragraph reinforces the thesis which emphasizes the fact that hard work pays off eventually and results in success and fame.

Here is another sample for writing an outline:

Ideas (brainstorming): My 4th grade students do not like math and I have hard time teaching it. I have found a good idea on the internet about using songs in teaching math. And I also tell the students to role-play to do simple math problems. At the end, the students show enjoyment in my class, and I become excited with my new teaching strategies.

Outline:

Introduction: As fun as teaching can be, it is full of challenges.

Thesis: I have decided to search for better strategies in teaching math to make it more enjoyable to my students.

Body: - I find songs on the internet about math.

 - I use role-play to help my students with simple equations.

Conclusion: The new strategies I use improve teaching and make it more fun.

Picture 3 provides these elements in the sandwich format.

- As fun as teaching can be, it is full of challenges.
Thesis: I have decided to search for better strategies in teaching math to make it more enjoyable to my students

- I find songs on the internet about math.
- I use role-play to help my students with simple equations

- The new strategies I use in teaching improve it and make it more fun

Picture 3, elements of a paragraph about teaching math

As we can see, the sandwich format organizes the ideas and facilitates the writing process. Moreover, it helps the reader practice sub-reading skills such as skimming and scanning. For example, if the reader wants to know the main idea of the text, they can directly look at the end of the introductory section as it is the place where the main idea; i.e. the thesis is located.

The coming chapters provide more details on how to write a short paragraph and complete essays.

1.2. Conjunctions and Transitions

Before discussing writing a short paragraph, it is important to learn how to connect the sentences in a paragraph or essay. Conjunctions and transitions are used to link ideas and sentences together. First we will discuss conjunctions.

1.2.1. Conjunctions

A conjunction can be defined as a part of speech that connects two words, two phrases, or two clauses together. Conjunctions are classified into three types: coordinating conjunctions, correlative conjunctions, and subordinating conjunctions. Table 1, discusses these three types.

type	Function(s)	Examples	Example sentences
Coordinating conjunctions	To join two equal items or more. Their initials form the acronym FANBOYS	And, but, nor, for, or, so, yet	- She is an artist and her sister is a musician - He was loud but he said it accurately.
Correlative conjunctions	Used in pairs to coordinate two words, phrases, or clauses.	Both ... and, either ... or, neither ... nor, whether ... or, not only ... but also	- I can neither sketch nor draw. - Not only is the food great, the restaurant is near my work.
Subordinating conjunctions	Also referred to as subordinators, are used to connect a dependant clause to an independent one.	Before, after, though, although, even though, as long as, as soon as, as much as, so that, that, since, because, if, even if, in order that, lest, while, whether, unless, until, where, when	- Since you are staying longer, let's play chess. - Even if the scholarship covers the tuition, I am still responsible for the fees. - Although she did not get the job in the bookstore, she got the chance to volunteer in the public library on Wednesday afternoons.

Table 1, English conjunctions

The following are examples of how to join more than one sentence by the use of conjunctions.

1. You should study hard for the test. You may fail.

These two sentences can be joined into one sentence with a conjunction. The decision on which conjunction to use is based on the type of relationship that holds between the ideas included in these sentences. It is understood that not studying hard for the test can result in failing it. Therefore, failing the test only happens if not studying for it happens first. As a result, it is a preconditioned relationship in two sentences that can be joined by the use of either the coordinating conjunction *or*, or by a subordinating conjunctions such as *unless*.

- You should study hard for the test or you may fail.
- You may fail unless you study hard for the test.

2. This neighborhood is noisy. It is dangerous.

The adjectives *noisy* and *dangerous* are attributed to this neighborhood. The negative meaning that connects these two adjectives can join the two sentences into one by the use of a correlative conjunction such as *not only … but also*, or *both … and*.

- Not only is this neighborhood noisy, it is dangerous too.
- This neighborhood is both noisy and dangerous.

3. He gets an A in the assignment. He still needs to get an A in the final test to pass the course.

It can be seen from this sentence that passing the assignment alone does not guarantee passing the course. The two actions (passing the assignment and passing the test) need to be accomplished in order for the course to be passed. The subordinating conjunction *even if* can be applied in this case.

- Even if he gets an A in the assignment, he still needs to get an A in the final test to pass the course.

1.2.2. Transitions

Transition words are connectors that are used to joins ideas within or between sentences. Therefore, there are different kinds of transition words because there are different ideas expressed in writing. Transitions can be classified into the categories presented in table 2.

Category	Examples	Function(s)	Example sentences
To begin	First of all, to start up, to begin with, basically	To present an idea to start a composition	To begin with, classes start as early as 7:30 a.m.
Contrast	In contrast, however, but, nevertheless, on the contrary, on the other hand, contrary to, nonetheless, despite (of), even though, nevertheless.	To show contrast and/or opposition between one idea and another within or between sentences.	- *In contrast* to the United States, soccer sport is referred to as football in the rest of the word. - I love tennis *but* my friend loves golf.
Addition	Furthermore, also, additionally, in addition to, moreover, likewise.	To add more ideas related to a previously provided one(s).	- The city is small and clean; moreover, the rent is reasonably affordable. - Everybody was excited at the party; also the DJ played all our favorite music.

Cause/effect	Consequently, accordingly, therefore, in this/that case, as a result, thus, hence, for this/that reason	To signal causal relationship that holds between the ideas.	- The elevator is out of order; therefore, we will take the stairs. - Because of weather inclement, the game is cancelled.
To conclude	Generally, generally speaking, in conclusion, to sum up, in sum, based on the above discussion, in other words, it is understood that, it is taken that.	To provide the take-home message that wraps up the writing.	- In sum, all the parents support the new uniform policy. - It is taken that such a project is going to pay off generously and benefit every member in the community.

Table 2 Transition words examples and functions

The following are examples of transition words used to connect more than one sentence into one.

1. The building is very ancient. The building needs immediate reconstruction.

It is understood that there is a connection between the two ideas (the period of time this building has existed and the necessity to reconstruct it). This connection is a cause-and-effect one. In other words, the need to reconstruct the building stems from the fact that it is very old. The two sentences can become one sentence by using transition words that indicate cause and effect. For example:

-   The building is very ancient; therefore, it needs immediate reconstruction.

2. I had lunch half an hour ago. I am still hungry.

The relationship between the two sentences indicates opposition of two contrasting ideas. They can be connected into one sentence such as the following:

-   I had lunch half an hour ago; however, I am still hungry.

Transition words are used to connect paragraphs as well since their function is to connect the ideas not the sentences per se. Take a look at this short paragraph:

Every morning I walk for about half an hour. This exercise makes me active and ready for the day. After I drink a cup of coffee, I leave for work. I walk to the bus stop which is about seven minutes away from my apartment. It is not fun to wait for the bus because I do not like waiting.

This paragraph ends with the idea that the writer is not interested in waiting for the bus. In order to keep the sequence of ideas in the story, another idea that connects to the one that ends the previous paragraph is added. One suggestion is to provide information about an opposing positive side of waiting for the bus. Here is an example of what the next paragraph may look like:

However, I bring a book to read while waiting for the bus in order to use my time appropriately. Reading is a good idea because it distracts me from city noises and conversations held by other people at the bus stop. I usually finish two to three pages by the time the bus arrives.

As seen, the idea of not liking to wait for the bus is connected with the idea of reading to pass time while waiting. The next paragraph ends with a sentence that can be connected with another sentence to indicate an addition relationship. For example:

My name is Erin, I am a student in the College of Business but I plan to change to Culinary instead. The first reason why I want to change my major from business to culinary is because I love cooking. I specifically find my self-fulfillment in making dessert and garnishing the cake. Making roses from colored cream is very relaxing and engaging. Whenever we have a family event, I always step in to make dessert. In fact, I do not remember the last time my mother has bought a dessert from the bakery.

Erin wants to major in culinary

Now another reason is required to explain the change in her major. This requirement is understood from the phrase *the first reason* at the beginning of the previous paragraph. Here is an example of a possible second reason:

Moreover, I want to major in culinary because my mother's friend, who owns a restaurant, loves the cakes I make. This increases my chance of getting a job upon graduation. The restaurant is famous and successful, and it is located downtown not far away from my apartment. If I get a job in that restaurant I can ride my bike to work and save gas money. Also, there is a bookstore on the way to the restaurant so I can search cook books and keep myself updated.

The next skill to learn is how to paraphrase sentences. This skill is required when writing the introduction and conclusion of short paragraphs and long essays.

1.3. Paraphrasing Sentences

- Daughter: Mom, today at school I have learned that the lion is very loud, grows big beard, and sleeps all the time while his wife brings food and takes care of children.
- Mother: In other words, you have learned about your father!

Paraphrasing means *rephrasing*, i.e.; restating the message in different words. This skill is required in academic writing in order to avoid academic dishonesty such as plagiarism. Good paraphrasing does not mean replacing the text word by word; rather, it reflects the writer's ability to understand the meaning of the sentence(s) as a whole and rewrite it using their own words. In addition, good paraphrasing skills improve vocabulary leaning and expand knowledge of using collocations and different expressions. It also develops well-structured sentence building and overall writing style.

There are many strategies that can be applied when paraphrasing. They include: using synonyms, changing nouns to verbs and vise versa, using conjunctions/transitions, using definitions, and using clauses.

One common way to paraphrase is to use synonyms of key words. This can be affective at and within the sentence level where frequent exchange of words does not result in poor rephrasing. Take a look at this sentence:

1. Most people agree that the proposed plan to save the company from going out of business is not effective in the long run.

This sentence contains words that can be replaced with their synonyms. For example, the word *most* can be replaced by the phrase *the majority of*. Likewise, the word *proposed* can be replaced by the word *suggested*. The phrase *going out of business* can be replaced by the noun *bankruptcy*. The adjective *effective* is replaced by the adjective *efficient*. Finally, the phrase *in the long run* can be replaced by the phrase *in the future*. As a result, the paraphrased sentence looks like this one:

- The majority of people agree that the suggested plan to save the company from bankruptcy is not efficient in the future.

As can be seen, phrases are replaced by single words and vise versa. The most important elements to remember when paraphrasing are 1) to stick to the meaning, and 2) to avoid paraphrasing at single-item level, i.e.; not to paraphrase every single word. Sentence 2 is another example.

2. The reconstruction noises in the building next door did not disturb the employees during the staff meeting.

The phrase *reconstruction noises* can be rephrased to something like *the noises caused by the reconstruction work*. This means that it is not always necessary to use synonyms of single words or change parts of speech. The reason is that the main purpose of paraphrasing is to keep the same meaning; and this can be obtained with no need to alter all the words and phrases. As a result, the verb *disturb* can be replaced by the verb *annoy*, and it can be rephrased to its noun and the phrase become *did not cause disturbance*. Lastly, the phrase *during staff meeting* can be replaced by the phrase *while staff meeting was being held*. It follows that complete replacement of words is not necessary or advisable. Here is the paraphrased sentence to sentence 2:

- The noises caused by the reconstruction work in the building next door did not cause disturbance to the employees while staff meeting was being held.

The following are other examples of paraphrasing sentences:

3. Original: As a result, the students were more ready for the test than last time.
- Paraphrased: Therefore, the students were more prepared to take the test than the time before.

4. Original: The engineer has decided to finally design the new city hall provided that he gets to use the project as a model in the conference he will attend.
- Paraphrased: The engineer wants to design the new city hall building if he can use this design in the conference he intends to attend.

5. Original: the decision is Omar's to practice photography as a hobby, or to take photography classes and turn this hobby into a career.
- Paraphrase: It is up to Omar to choose between taking a college degree in photography, or perform photography as a hobby.

Omar loves photography

6. Original: Moreover, this class gives the students the opportunity to visit different farms and laboratories in order to help them with their papers for the finals.
- Paraphrased: In addition, the students in this class can work on their final papers by doing field studies in farms and laboratories.

7. Original: For Julia, taking revenge results in more negative energy and hatred.
- Paraphrased: Julia believes that vindictive reactions intensify negative energy and entrench hatred.

8. Original: The slogan of this campaign is based on the perspective that resoluteness is the drive to perseverance and continuation.
- Paraphrased: This campaign has a motto to emphasize the fact that determination motivates perseverance and perpetuation.

9. Original: What I want to say is that the program is not going to start until late December, and this allows for more preparation.

- - Paraphrased: In other words, the program will start late December, which gives us time for extra planning.

Chapter 4 provides discussion about paraphrasing longer paragraphs when writing summaries.

Exercise1. Organize the following ideas into an introduction/ a body/ and a conclusion to construct a writing format.

1. Sarah is looking for an apartment near campus because she walks to class and she has early classes. She searches for a roommate because she cannot afford apartment rent, but she still cannot find a roommate.

2. Omar decides to start a new business in real estate, and he has little experience in this field. After going through a hard time, he manages to get the hang of it and makes it through his new business in real estate. He used to have a restaurant, so changing business is not easy for him.

Omar starts a real states business

3. The building needs maintenance for a long time because almost all services are disabled due to the huge malfunction that the building goes through. The semester starts in two weeks so scheduling for maintenance at this time is completely inappropriate.

4. Students in the school say that the physics textbook is so intense and hard to understand. The teachers want to help the students grasp the material thoroughly. The teachers decide to schedule after-school workshops three days a week. The teachers also decide to skip the last chapter in the book to make things easier for the students. It is hard work for teachers and students but they manage to do it.

5. The Robinsons need to either go camping or go to the beach for their next vacation. The weather is nice so the beach sounds like a good idea. But they have been to the beach before, and they have never gone camping. They have all the equipments for camping. They decide to go camping.
6. The owner of the property decides to build a house on it. There is a big three in the middle of the property. The owner first decides to cut it off but the engineer suggests designing the house with the tree included in the design because this is original and nature-friendly. The owner agrees.

Exercise 2. Connect the two sentences in the following examples into one sentence by using the appropriate transition words.

1. Zuhair studies in the college of Dentistry because he wants to become a successful dentist after he graduates. He works in a dentist clinic every weekend in order to get more experience in his major of specialty.

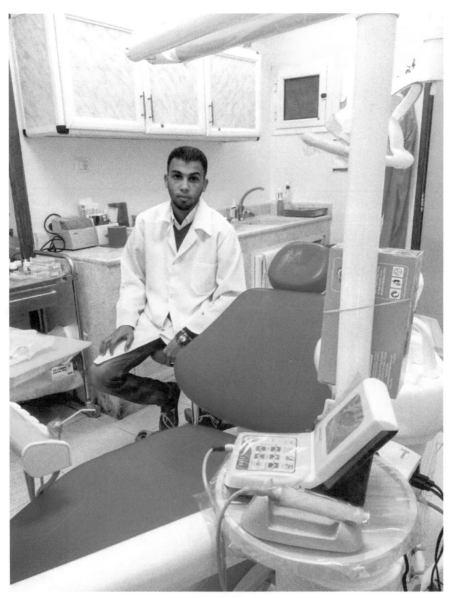

Zuhair is a student in Dentistry

14

2. The government is not considering raising taxes. The citizens demand tax raise.
3. Helen was sick in the morning. She insisted to go to her class.
4. The party will have Hollywood celebrity theme. A picture of Johnny Depp will be on the cake.
5. The police officer saw her speeding. He did not stop her.
6. She noticed her old pants do not fit any more. She decided to start working out.
7. They need to buy a new car. Their old car hardly gets them anywhere.
8. I need to enroll in a class that does not require a lot of work and essay writing. I am thinking of taking a language class this semester.
9. Playing the piano used to be a hobby for me. I now think of making it a way to get extra cash.
10. He needs to spend more quality time with his son. He registers in a karate class with his son.

Exercise 3. The following sentences are incomplete. Based on the functions of the transition words used in each point, complete the rest of sentences to give them full meaning.

1. I first want to make tabula for a snack but I've run out of tomatoes; as a result, ……..
2. She is the first in her class every year, and …………………………….
3. This house is smaller than the last one, far away from campus and ……………..
4. Since you have no idea about the program you intend to apply for, ………………..
5. I am afraid I have no time to either do this again or …………………………..
6. All the people in group A disagree with the new proposal; group B, in contrast, …………
7. The patient's family are concerned that the surgery may not be successful, and they keep asking the doctor many questions. As a result, the doctor …………………..
8. They did not approve the document because it was faxed for signature instead of the person coming physically to sign it. Consequently, …………

Exercise 4. Paraphrase the following sentences

1. It is the desire of our company that the partnership future track with your company is not interrupted by minor misfortunes.
2. My card is stuck in the ATM probably because I entered the wrong Pin Number.
3. Due to inclement weather, the tourism agency has canceled the trip until a further notice.
4. Owning a horse is the dream of many people; however, few are aware of the hard work, care, and money demanded when having a horse.
5. It is advisable that you keep the drive on your person should you need to work on your paper whenever and wherever is convenient.
6. Mustafa is currently a free-lance writer to a number of journals; but he decides to have his own writing business so he intends to design an online journal.

Mustafa is a free-lance writer

7. Although the manager will not be able to give the speech or even attend the event, the grand opening ceremony will still take place on time.
8. She has decided to practice soccer and become professional because she needs a sports scholarship to get a college admission.
9. The idea is that we need more referrals for our business to become well-known.
10. The teacher has finally decided to extend the deadline to submit the paper for two more days.

Chapter Two

Building a Paragraph

"No army can withstand the strength
of an idea whose time has come"
Victor Hugo

Paragraph writing goes under the same outline longer essays do. They include an introduction, a body, and a conclusion. Figure (2) illustrates the steps of writing a paragraph

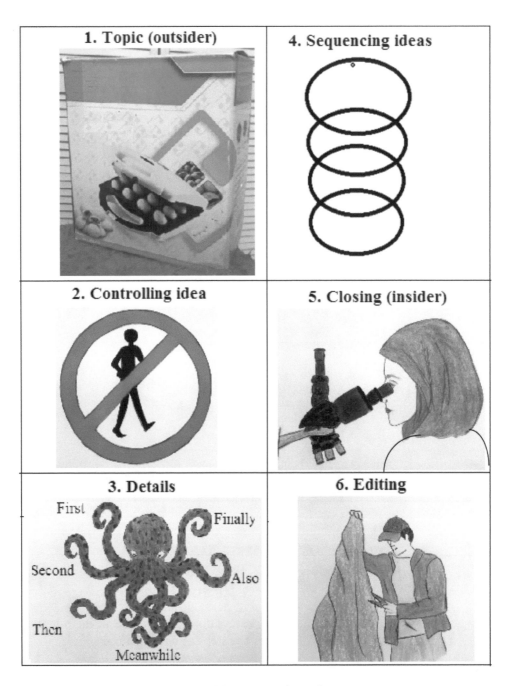

Figure (2) Paragraph outline

As indicated in Figure (2), there are six major steps into writing a paragraph:

1. Topic (outsider): once the topic is chosen, the writer first has a general outsider view of it with no details included. As the Figure 2 shows, we know from the outside of the box that it is an appliance used in the kitchen. However, we cannot tell for sure what kind of food it can be used for. Such information requires us to open the box and read the instruction book in order to learn more about the details. Therefore, the topic part is very general and needs to be tackled from one perspective only; namely, the controlling idea.

2. Controlling idea: It is the specific aspect of the topic that we intend to cover in the writing. It is called the controlling idea because it controls the writer to that aspect under discussion only. The topic and

the controlling idea constitute the main idea of the paragraph. This main idea is referred to as the *topic sentence*. More details are provided below.

3. Details: the writer includes the details that are connected to the topic sentence. Details which are not related to the controlling idea are not included even if they are within the domain of the topic. For example, if the topic is about the advantages of living in a particular city, the writer should not bring up discussion about pollution because pollution is not an advantage. As depicted in the octopus in figure (2), all the details should be connected to the topic sentence the same way the legs are connected to the octopus' head.

4. Sequencing ideas: It is important that the ideas in supporting sentences flaw smoothly not just in sequence of events, but also in connecting them by using transition words. More details are provided below.

5. Closing (Take-home message): After all the details are provided in the supporting sentences, the writer has an insider view of the topic. Therefore, it can be wrapped up in the concluding sentence.

6. Editing: This step is important in any kind of writing. The writer needs to make sure the paragraph does not have any errors. The C.U.P.S. strategy can be a good one to use in editing. C.U.P.S. stands for *Capitalization*, *Usage*, *Punctuation*, and *Spelling*. All these elements must be checked in order to make sure they are used correctly in the paragraph.

2.1. Steps in Writing a Paragraph

Prior to developing an outline, a topic must be chosen. For students, the topic can also be assigned to them by their teacher. Once the topic is chosen, the next step is to brainstorm ideas about it. So by virtue, brainstorming can be the actual first step in writing the first draft. But what is brainstorming?

2.1 .1 Brainstorming

When you decide to write about a topic, the next step is to think of as many ideas as you can get about it. You can think of nouns, adjectives, phrases or even idioms that have a certain relation to that topic. For example, if the assigned topic is *summer vacation*, you can brainstorm words such as: hot, beach, tickets, refreshments, travelling, family, swimming, cold beverages, having fun, barbeque, flip flops, sunglasses, weather umbrella, breeze, trip, warm, cook, sunny, hotel reservation, party, cool, towel, music, tanning, waves, mist, ice cream, playing, melon.

Of course not every single word has to be used in the paragraph. The purpose of brainstorming step is to make sure the topic is tackled from as many aspects as possible. After writing everything you can think of about the topic, you choose the words and/or phrases that are related to what you want to talk about in the topic. There are many ways in organizing words by categorizing them in subject trees, clustering, lists, and outlines. Here are examples of each one.

Summer Vacation

```
              Summer Vacation
              /            \
        Family time        Beach
         /      \          /      \
   Barbeque    Party   Swimming   Weather
    /    \      /   \      |    \        \
Refreshments Cook Beverages Music Tanning Sunglasses  Hot
```

The topic is written in the big central circle

Then more ideas are added in other circles attached to the central one.

And then more details are added to the ideas.

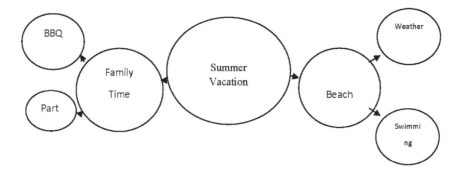

More circles are added as needed to cover the main idea.

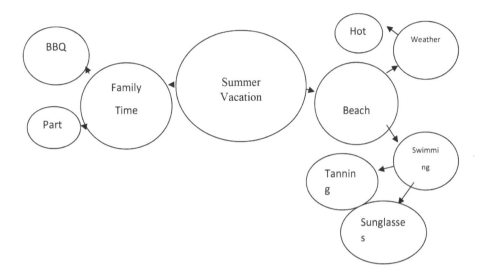

Lists

In Lists, the words are organized in terms of a certain category. For example, if the category is parts of speech, then we have a list for nouns, a list for verbs, a list for adjectives, etc. such as the list below:

Summer Vacation

NOUNS	VERBS	ADJECTIVES
Family time	Tanning	Hot
Barbeque	Swimming	Cold
Party		Warm
Beach		Sunny
Weather		Cool
Swimming		
Sunglasses		

Outline

The outline format is common in academic writing. It includes organizing the words in Roman numeral lists.

I. Introduction

   a. Attention getter
   b. Thesis

II. Body

   a. Family time
   1. Barbeque
   2. Party

21

        a.   Beach
        1.   Weather
        i.   hot
        ii. Swimming
        iii. Tanning
        iv. Sunglasses

III. Conclusion

        a.   Thesis restatement

It should be brought to attention that writing full introductory and concluding sentences is not required in the brainstorming step. As a personal favorite of mine, I like to postpone writing them until I am done with the body section. More discussion on how to write the introduction and conclusion is provided next.

2. 2. Introduction

The introduction in a paragraph consists of the attention getter and the thesis. Although the attention getter is placed before the topic sentence in writing outline, forming a good one depends on knowing the topic and the controlling idea; therefore, it is formed after the topic sentence is constructed.

2. 2.1. Thesis (main idea)

After organizing your vocabulary in a certain category, you need to develop the main idea of your composition. The main idea is what your whole writing is connected to. In other words, all other sentences/paragraphs discuss details related to the main idea. The main idea in academic writing is referred to as the thesis or topic sentence. The thesis has two components: the topic and the controlling idea.

2. 2.2. How to form a Thesis

The discussion now moves to forming the main idea. Let's take the topic above as an example; *Summer Vacation*. This topic generally implies positive ideas. Accordingly, the words generated in the brainstorming step express a general positive attitude towards summer vacation. For instance, if we take a look at the nouns chosen we notice that selecting them is based on a positive background idea about summer (e.g. party, beach, barbeque, travelling, ice cream, music). Likewise, the verbs chosen reflect pleasurable actions (e.g. swimming, tanning, playing, and having fun). Adjectives also describe positive attitudes towards summer (e.g. cool, warm, and sunny).

As a result, it is understood that the writer likes summer vacation, and wants to talk positively about it. Based on the ideas in the brainstorming step, the fun is limited to family time and going to the beach. As a result, the main idea is formed in a sentence like this one:

Summer vacation is the time when I have fun with my family and go to the beach

We understand from this topic sentence that the topic is about summer vacation. Moreover, it can be predicted that the next sentences provide description of the writer's activities in the summer. And we know that the writer will talk about positive things only, because the topic sentence includes the word *fun* which restricts the writer to write only about positive things. This restriction is referred to as *controlling idea*.

2. 2.3. Components of the Topic Sentence.

As understood from the topic sentence above, the topic sentence consists of two components: the topic and the control idea.

Topic + control idea = Topic sentence.

The topic *summer vacation* is tackled from one perspective; namely, the time when I have fun. Accordingly, the phrase *the time when I have fun* is the controlling idea. No matter how many negative aspects summer vacation has, the writer cannot talk about them in this piece of writing because the controlling idea limits the discussion about the topic to be about the fun things only.

2. 2.4. General vs. Specific Topic Sentences

The controlling idea in the topic sentence should not be too specific or too general. In other words, it should thoroughly cover a specific aspect of the topic. Take a look at this topic sentence:

There are many difficulties in our daily life.

This sentence includes an idea that is too broad. The difficulties people go through in their life are infinite, and can never fit in a small paragraph or even a longer essay. Such a sentence can function as an introductory statement of the paragraph but it cannot function as a topic sentence. Likewise, the following sentence is not suitable as a topic sentence because it is too specific:

I spend Saturday afternoons watching TV.

As seen, this sentence is too narrow to be a topic sentence because no more details can be added to it. However, a sentence such as, *I do some activities on Saturday*; can function as a topic sentence because details about the kinds of activities, which include watching TV can be added. Table 3 includes examples of general and specific ideas.

Specific	General
Integrity Honesty Generosity	Good qualities
Paper cut Computer crash Unloaded printer	Mishaps at work
Stealing lunch money Gossiping Creating funny nicknames	Bullying at school
Doing the dishes Doing the laundry Taking out the trash	Undesired chores
Too many pieces of jewelry High heels Heavy makeup	Overly dressed

Table 3, specific and general ideas

The general ideas provided in Table 3 can be used to form the opening statement when writing a paragraph or an essay. For example:

- Good qualities are admired by everyone. Some of the qualities that are sought in every individual include integrity, honesty, and generosity.
- We always hear people complain about undesired chores that have to be done nevertheless. People see tasks such as doing the dishes, doing the laundry, and taking out the trash really boring and undesired.

The following are examples of topic sentence that are not too specific or too general.

1. I am not a big fan of tennis.

This sentence indicates that this person does not like to play tennis. Therefore, if it is used as a topic sentence in a paragraph, the topic is tennis; i.e. the discussion is about tennis only, not other sport or anything else. The controlling idea is the phrase *I am not a big fan*. This person does not like tennis so the supporting sentences in the body section of the paragraph give reasons why this person dislikes tennis. Examples of these reasons could be because tennis is an exhausting sport, or that it requires a high level of focus, or that it works better with individuals who are more athletically fit, etc.

2. There are three advantages in living in this city

The topic of this sentence is *living in this city*, and the controlling idea is *there are three advantages*. The supporting sentences should include three positive aspects about the given city because the controlling idea restricts the discussion to advantages only. Including at least one disadvantage violates the controlling idea, also including more than three advantages is inappropriate.

2. 2. 5. Attention Getter (Hook)

Attention getter, also known as the hook, is a sentence that is placed first in the paragraph in the form of a statement or question. The purpose of the attention getter is to get the readers' attention and make them interested in reading the paragraph.

If you want to add an attention getter to the paragraph *summer vacation*, it has to be something attractive to the reader and related to the topic. For example, a sentence such as *What a summer I had!* can be a good start to your paragraph because it makes the reader curious to know more about that summer. Another example is a sentence like *You know how it gets in summer,* which also motivates the reader to keep reading. As noticed, the attention getter does not include keywords that signal positive or negative opinions because we need the reader to keep reading in order to explore the idea the writer has about the topic.

Now that we have the thesis available, *Summer vacation is the time when I have fun with my family and go to the beach* and the attention getter is also ready, we can start working on the introductory part of the paragraph. The following is an example:

What a summer I had! I always wait for summer to come to do many activities with my family. Summer vacation is the time when I have fun with my family and go to the beach.

The next step is structuring the supporting sentences. More details in the following section.

2.3 Supporting Sentences

Supporting sentences in a short paragraph form the body section. They include more details about the information provided in the main idea (the thesis). The number of supporting sentences in a short paragraph usually ranges from three to five sentences, and they include all the components of the thesis.

The thesis of the topic *Summer Vacation* includes two activities: having fun with family and going to the beach. Accordingly, the body section should have sentences about spending time with family and other sentences about spending time at the beach.

Having fun with family

Before discussing details about this point, a topic sentence that represents introductory part of this supporting detail should be constructed. The purpose is for the reader to know what the writer is going to talk about. And since the words selected in brainstorming stage regarding family time are *barbeque* and *party*, we need to restrict our sentence to these two points. Here is an example.

Family time in summer is a wonderful opportunity to have barbeques and parties.

Now that we have our topic sentence ready, we can write two sentences about these points. Let's make a sentence about having barbeque with family. Note that all sentences must imply positive information because that is the controlling idea of the topic. For example:

Our Friday barbeque every two weeks is family time to catch up and enjoy the food.

Now we need a sentence about having a party. And again always remember that you like summer vacation so all the sentences you write must have indications to that attitude. Here is an example sentence:

We have big parties in which we play different games and eat cake.

Now, we have sentences about the barbeque and the party ready. However, we still need to connect them by using an appropriate transition word. In order to know what transition word to use, we need to understand the connection between *barbeque* and *party*. Why do we talk about them in this paragraph? Because we want to explain how we have fun in the summer. Accordingly, we know that *barbeque* and *party* are details of having fun in the summer; and therefore, the best transition word to use is the one that provides the meaning of addition (e.g. in addition, additionally, furthermore, moreover, and also). And now we can link the details about having family time by using a transition word, for example:

Family time in summer is a wonderful opportunity to have barbeque and parties. Our Friday barbeque every two weeks is family time to catch up and enjoy the food. In addition, we have big parties in which we play different games and eat cake.

Now that the first supporting detail is structured, the next step is to write sentences related to the second supporting detail; the beach. First we need an introductory topic sentence such as this one:

Summer is beach time

This sentence needs to be preceded by a transition word because it continues the discussion of summer vacation activities. A transition word such as *furthermore* can be used.

Furthermore, summer is beach time.

In the brainstorming stage, we plan to talk about the *weather* and *swimming*. In this regard, one sentence for each point is formed. We need to include the adjective 'hot' when constructing the sentence about the weather because it is provided in the outline. We can have a sentence like this one:

We enjoy the hot weather at the beach.

And finally, we need one last sentence to talk about swimming, with the words *tanning* and *sunglasses* included.

I like swimming and my brother likes tanning and wearing sunglasses.

The last sentence to form now is the concluding sentence.

2.4. Conclusion

The concluding sentence wraps up the paragraph. As discussed in chapter one, the concluding sentence generally includes the information covered in the introductory sentence only in different words. The thesis of this paragraph is 'summer vacation is the time when I have fun with my family and go to the beach'. This sentence needs to be paraphrased to form the concluding sentence. Here is an example:

I love going to the beach and spending time with my family during the summer.

Now we have all the sentences ready, we can put them together to have one complete paragraph like this one:

What a summer I had! I always wait for summer to come to do many activities with my family. Summer vacation is the time when I have fun with my family and go to the beach. Family time in summer is a wonderful opportunity to have barbeque and parties. Our Friday barbeque every two weeks is family time to catch up and enjoy the food. In addition, we have big parties in which we play different games and eat cake. Furthermore, summer is beach time. We enjoy the hot weather at the beach. I like swimming and my brother likes tanning and wearing sunglasses. I love going to the beach and spending time with my family during the summer.

Once you finish writing, you need to go through your paragraph again in order to make sure you do not have any grammar and/or punctuation mistakes. It is advisable that your ask someone else to read it for you to make sure your paragraph is error-free.

2.5. Sample Paragraph One

Here is another example of a short paragraph. The paragraph is about the cousins Deyazen and Omar who are big fans of soccer.

Deyazen and his cousin Omar

- Topic: soccer
- Brainstorming: love soccer, cousins Deyazen and Omar, ball, playing, watch games, World Cup, soccer fans, practice.
- Outline:

I. Introduction.

a. Thesis: the cousins Deyazen and Omar love soccer

II. Body

a. Supporting idea: They watch their fathers play soccer.

b. Supporting idea: They join the city soccer team.

c. Supporting idea: They look up to famous soccer models.

III. Conclusion.

Paragraph

Soccer has always been a passionate sport for many people all over the world. One example is the cousins Deyazen and Omar who love soccer so much. They grew up watching their fathers play soccer and consequently fell in love with it. As adults, they watch soccer games and have a serious discussion about them after they finish. Moreover, they are players in the city soccer team and therefore have the chance to practice it most of the time. In addition, they have famous soccer players as role models from whom they learn about how to be really smart and skillful in this game. They dream to become famous soccer players worldwide and have fans of their own. Indeed soccer is an international game that has huge audience in every county.

2.6. Sample Paragraph Two

- Topic: Being an excellent student
- Brainstorming: study, tests, straight A, ask the teacher, group study, time management, punctuality.
- Outline:

I. Introduction.

a. Thesis: There are several strategies a student takes in order to become an excellent student.

II. Body

a. Supporting idea: time management

b. Supporting idea: group studies

c. Supporting idea: Ask the teacher

III. Conclusion.

Paragraph

Being a student means facing challenges which increase when the student seeks higher grades. There are several strategies a student takes in order to become an excellent student. One strategy is related to time management. In order for students to become good at their school work, they need to organize their time and never procrastinate in doing their assignments or preparing for tests. A second strategy to become a good student is to join group studies with other students. Studying with classmates helps the student become more focused on the important points in the textbook and the points the teacher refers to in class. Finally, an excellent student always asks the teacher questions in class and in office hours. The teacher remembers students who ask questions all the time and this is likely to result in overcoming minor mistakes those students make in the test. In sum, following these strategies have positive results to make students become excellent and get high grades.

2.7. Sample Paragraph Three

- Topic: Social media
- Brainstorming: interactions, chatting with family/friends, posting, block, newsfeed, link, share, tag, send message, photos, and video
- Outline:

I. Introduction.

a. Thesis: Social media has brought families and friends closer.

II. Body

    a. Supporting idea: updates from family and friends

    b. Supporting idea: share pictures and videos

    c. Supporting idea: make new friends

III. Conclusion.

Paragraph

With the increasing advancement of technology, human communication has become easier and more versatile. One service provided by technology is social media. Social media has brought families and friends closer. It is easier now to get updates about loved ones despite the physical distances. Also, social media has made it possible to share photos and videos with family and friends and enjoy having conversations about these posts. Moreover, social media is another way to make new friends. In some cases, these friendships extend to the real world and friends meet each other face to face. Generally speaking, the more technology we have, the smaller the world becomes and the easier it gets to bond with family and friends.

2.8. Constructing Multiple Controlling Ideas for One Topic

There is more than one aspect to talk about in different topics. The more aspects of a topic are discussed the more the topic is covered thoroughly. In this case, we can have more than one controlling idea for a single topic. For example, if the topic is camping, the writer can talk about how they love camping and give examples of their camping trips, or the writer talks about how they hate camping and give reasons for that. The following are examples of writing short paragraphs about the same topic but from two different aspects.

2. 8.1. Paragraph One (living in small city)

-    Topic: Living in a small city
-    Brainstorming: quiet, affordable rent, less pollution, less traffic, better schools, less job opportunities, less recreation areas, affordable private tutoring, beautiful nature.
-    Outline:

I. Introduction.

    a. Thesis: Living in a small city is a good option for families.

II. Body

    a. Supporting idea: better schools

    b. Supporting idea: affordable private tutoring

    c. Supporting idea: beautiful nature

III. Conclusion.

Paragraph

The desire to live in small cities is on the increase especially among young families that seek healthy lifestyles. Living in a small city is a good option for families. First, families seek better schools for their children. They want schools that are safe, secure and have less bullying incidents. Also, providing private tutoring for children is more affordable in a small city. Parents can enroll their children in sports classes, dance classes and music classes. Additionally, there is more chance to enjoy the beautiful nature in a small city. Families can go camping, hiking, and fishing which is a good chance for bonding with each other. Families prefer living in a small city as they find it more appealing to their needs.

- Topic: Living in a small city.
- Brainstorming: quiet, affordable rent, less pollution, less traffic, better schools, less job opportunities, less recreation areas, less public transportation, affordable private tutoring, beautiful nature.
- Outline:

I. Introduction.

a. Thesis: Young individuals do not prefer to live in a small city.

II. Body

a. Supporting idea: less job opportunities

b. Supporting idea: less recreation areas

c. Supporting idea: less public transportation

III. Conclusion.

Paragraph

Although living in small cities is more demanded among families, young individuals do not prefer to live in a small city. The first reason is that there are less job opportunities in small cities than there are in big cities. College students need to have part-time jobs in order to afford their rent and living expenses. Moreover, young people want to enjoy their free time in different recreation areas which are not always available in smaller cities. For example, going to the gym and going bowling with friends in weekends is fun, more affordable and less time consuming than traveling out of the city to have fun. Lastly, big cities have more public transportation services than small cities. People use public transportation in order to save gas money and not to worry about where to park. Young adults find it more appealing to live in a big city because it serves their needs more than living in a small city.

2. 8.2. Paragraph Two (soccer)

The second example provides two paragraphs about soccer; each paragraph tackles the topic from two different aspects.

- Topic: Soccer

- Brainstorming: ball, kick, shootouts, penalty kicks, players, goalkeeper, win, World Cup, big fans, popular, family time, friendship, dream career.
- Outline:

I. Introduction.

a. Thesis: Soccer is a popular sport that is played with a team of players and a ball and has certain rules.

II. Body

a. Supporting idea: Team

b. Supporting idea: rules

c. Supporting idea: events

III. Conclusion.

Paragraph

Soccer is one of the very well-known sports that have big fans around the world. Soccer, also called association football, is a popular sport that is played with a team of players and a ball and has certain rules. This sport is practiced by a group of athletes referred to as players. The number of players in each team is eleven, with other substitute players stay ready in case a switch is required during the game. There is a player called goalkeeper whose job is to guard the goal line from the ball kicked by the other team. In addition, the goalkeeper is the only player who is allowed to touch the ball with their hands for few seconds. The decision about which team to start the first kick-off is made by flipping a coin. After one team scores, the other team takes the next kick-off. The team that has the higher number of scores by the end of the game time wins the game. In case of a tie, shootouts are played until one of the teams wins. Soccer is played in different international sports events including the Olympics. It has its own big event which is called the World Cup that takes place every four years. Although soccer is more popular among men, there are female soccer teams that are famous and successful as well. This sport is hugely popular in many countries and is the number one sport in some countries.

- Topic: Soccer
- Brainstorming: ball, kick, shootouts, penalty kicks, players, goalkeeper, win, World Cup, big fans, popular, family time, friendship, dream career.
- Outline:

I. Introduction.

a. Thesis: Soccer is the sport that constitutes family time in our household.

II. Body

a. Supporting idea: bonding with family

b. Supporting idea: play soccer

c. Supporting idea: become professional

III. Conclusion.

Paragraph

Not only is soccer a popular sport all over the world, it is popular in our house too. Soccer is the sport that constitutes family time in our household. Watching soccer games is our family bonding time. Everybody in my family gathers in front of the TV and cheers our team enthusiastically. We also have conversations after the game to talk about the player's performance. Every weekend, we play soccer with friends and we make small competitions that follow the World Cup rules. We have ceremonies and a cup that we make from recycled foam cups painted in gold color. My brother and I have a dream to become successful and famous soccer players in the future, and the support we receive from my family is tremendous. I am so happy the whole family has a passion in soccer that keeps us all connected to each other.

2. 8.3. Paragraph Three (China)

The next two paragraphs describe two different aspects about China.

- Topic: China
- Brainstorming: economy, nature, tourism, innovation, population, science technology, sport, auto technology, nature, Great Wall of China, food.
- Outline:

I. Introduction.

a. Thesis: Economy in China is constantly growing due to increasing technological developments in different fields.

II. Body

a. Supporting idea: electronic technology

b. Supporting idea: space technology

c. Supporting idea: energy

III. Conclusion.

Paragraph

China is a very rich country in resources and history which roots back to thousands of years. Additionally, it has one of the most powerful economies in the world. Economy in China is constantly growing due to increasing technological developments in different fields. For example, one cause of recent economy growth in China is its electronic technology that has spread all over the world. China manufactures TVs, mobile phones, monitors, computers, etc. Furthermore, China is also active in space technology. They send satellites to the space and have recently launched a radio telescope which is the largest in the world. The industry of power generation in China is developing as well. There are attempt to use natural resources such as coal in the near future as an alternative power source. China is deeply rooted in the past and is no doubt deeply rooted in the future of technology.

- Topic: China
- Brainstorming: economy, nature, tourism, innovation, population, science technology, sport, auto technology, nature, Great Wall of China, food.
- Outline:

I. Introduction.

a. Thesis: China is one of the best places to visit when you decide to travel for tourism.

II. Body

a. Supporting idea: nature

b. Supporting idea: historical site

c. Supporting idea: food

III. Conclusion.

Paragraph

Deciding where to travel for tourism is not an easy decision to make. However, there are places that must be visited whenever there is a chance to. China is one of the best places to visit when you decide to travel for tourism. One good feature about travelling to China is the country's nature. China has beautiful natural sites in which tourists enjoy lakes, forests, mountains, valleys and wonderful greenery. Another good aspect about China is its wonderful historical sites. The Great Wall of China is by no doubt China's greatest historical icon. There are other historical buildings such as Temple of Heaven, Potala Palace, and Forbidden City among other buildings. The Chinese cuisine is another good reason to visit China. Chinese food is characterized by the smell, taste and color of the food. Also, seasoning is a key ingredient in Chinese food. In addition, tourists always like to use chopsticks to eat Chinese food. China is an inevitable option to consider when it comes to planning for tourism.

2.9. Constructing Different Controlling Ideas

In most cases, the controlling ideas are recycled over and over in writing classes. For example, if the teacher assigns a topic such as smoking, the students very likely construct a controlling idea that indicates how harmful smoking is. Likewise, a paragraph about birthday parties involves the positive aspects of this event and the joy it brings to people. Such predictions result in thinking fossilization which hinders creativity and critical thinking. Therefore, there is a need to develop creative thinking in order to improve academic writing skills. It is important that the students realize the fact that there are two sides (or more) for ever story, and sticking to one side always gives part of the truth. Improving these skills is specifically significant at the advanced levels of academic writing when students write argumentative essays.

Our knowledge about something is processed in a certain pattern that is abstract and restricted to previously established judgments. The process of arranging the knowledge in a new pattern is referred to as *thinking*. According to the Maltese thinker Edward De Bono (1985)[1], there are differences between traditional

---

[1] De Bono, E. (1985). Conflicts: a better way to resolve them. Penguin Group, European Music Ltd.

thinking and creative thinking. In traditional thinking, the hypothesis is already fossilized and therefore judgments are produced. Creative thinking, on the other hand, focuses on provocations of new ideas from familiar topics, especially those that are used to be regarded traditionally, and generate a new movement of thinking. This difference can be depicted as follows:

Traditional thinking → Hypothesis → Judgment

Creative thinking → Provocation → Movement

One suggestion to improve creative thinking skills is to tackle familiar topics from new aspects in order to create topic sentences which are different from what we are used to discuss. By discussing the two topics mentioned above; i.e. smoking and birthday parties, they can be discussed in different ways. For example, instead of thinking about the disadvantages of smoking, the controlling idea focuses on the advantages of smoking as seen by smokers. Possible advantages of smoking include: less talking, weight loss, looking more mature, keeping real friends who can stand the smell, etc. On the other hand, some disadvantages of birthday parties are expenses, getting older, unhealthy food, etc.

One interesting example is the common belief that a comma saves life. We are all familiar with the famous statement *let's eat grandma* that puts our beloved grandma into danger until the comma comes to the rescue, *let's eat, grandma*, and changes the statement's meaning from a suggestion to eat grandma into a suggestion to eat with grandma. In this regard, if the teacher asks students to write a short paragraph about the use of commas, all students say that a comma is a very important punctuation mark because it saves lives. However, there are times in which using a comma does not save lives. Take a look at these examples:

- Would you like me to cut you, a piece of cake?
- Let's throw her, a birthday party!
- My father always beats me, in chess!

As we can see in these examples, using a comma changes the meaning completely and omitting it is the only way to save lives. It follows that it is wise to relate everything to the context in hand and avoid making general absolute judgments because everything is contextual. Developing this skill at the intermediate level of academic writing proficiency plays an important role in improving argumentative essay writing at the advanced level.

Below are examples of how to write short paragraphs about the new controlling ideas for the two topics discussed above; i.e. smoking and birthdays, in addition to other topics.

2.9.1. Paragraph One (the advantages of smoking for smokers)

- Topic: Smoking
- Brainstorming: harmful to health, family, expensive, second-hand smokers, smoke, cough, yellow teeth, lose weight, talk less, looks mature, select good friends.
- Outline:

I. Introduction.

a. Thesis: Smoking has many advantages for those who smoke.

II. Body

    a. Supporting idea: helps losing weight

    b. Supporting idea: reduces talking time

    c. Supporting idea: maintains true friends

III. Conclusion.

Paragraph

It is commonsense that smoking has harmful effects in the smoker's physical, financial and social life. Nevertheless, there are people who smoke and find it hard to quit despite their awareness of the harmful results smoking eventually brings. Smoking has many advantages for those who smoke. The reason is that smoking serves a number of purposes for smokers. One possible reason is that smoking helps losing weight. Even thought this weight loss is not totally healthy, it can be appealing to some smokers. Smokers also talk less than non-smokers, partly because their mouths are busy with smoking and because smoking is more enjoyable when smokers focused on it and not get distracted by talking. Finally, smokers believe that smoking keeps good friends who are ready and willing to put up with the smell and other undesirable manners that result from smoking. It follows that there are some positive outcomes smoking brings to smokers in addition to being dangerous to their health and financial and social lives.

2.9.2. Paragraph Two (disadvantages of birthday parties)

- Topic: Birthday parties
- Brainstorming: presents, candles, cake, balloons, party, family, friends, gift card, surprise, cupcakes, goodie bag.
- Outline:

I. Introduction.

    a. Thesis: There are many disadvantages in celebrating birthdays.

II. Body

    a. Supporting idea: unhealthy food

    b. Supporting idea: expenses

    c. Supporting idea: one year older

III. Conclusion.

Paragraph

Birthdays are a big event that is recognized and celebrated all over the world regardless of the person's age as it is time to have a party and eat cake with friends and family and enjoy their gifts. Moreover, the birthday person gets angry of his/her loved ones if they forget about the birthday. However, what birthday people seem not to pay attention to is the fact that there are many disadvantages in celebrating birthdays. The first is eating unhealthy food. Birthday cakes are full of calories, fat, and sugar. Plus, the juice served is in most cases colored water with sugar. These factors increase the chance of gaining weight and having health problems such as diabetes. The second disadvantage of birthday parties is the amount of money put in them. Some well-off families allocate a big budget to throw birthday parties for their kids; for example, they order cater services from expensive restaurants and bring a band and a little Pony to ride. Even if the party is small with little unhealthy food, there is still the fact that the birthday person is actually celebrating getting one year older. Although this may not be an issue to children and younger people, it may be alarming for older fellows especially those who desire to accomplish recognizable achievements in their life. Birthday parties, though the time when we have joy and fun, are also the time when we ignore our health, spend a lot of money and try to recollect our achievements in the year that has past.

2.9.3. Paragraph Three (disconnect to socialize)

- Topic: disconnect to socialize
- Brainstorming: Taha, go outdoors, adventure, exotic, nowhere, connect with nature, enjoy, understand the world, appreciation, thankful, love civilization, love others.
- Outline:

I. Introduction.

a. Thesis: Taha believes it is important to disconnect from human world in order to socialize better with humans

II. Body

a. Supporting idea: stop taking things for granted

b. Supporting idea: appreciation

c. Supporting idea: get more inner peace

III. Conclusion.

Taha loves the outdoors

Paragraph

It is always fun to travel to exotic places in the outdoors and live the adventure of disconnecting from civilization. Taha believes it is important to disconnect from human world in order to socialize better with humans. Being in touch with humans on a daily basis can result in taking things for granted. In other words, getting used to seeing family and friends everyday may lead to underestimate the role their presence plays in our lives. According to Taha, going to the middle of nowhere makes him feel like a stranger who needs to reunite with loved ones. This consequently teaches him to appreciate himself and others more. Staying in the outdoors gives Taha the chance to live the feeling of being missed and remembered. When he receives messages from his family and friends asking about him, he knows that he is important to them as much as they are important to him. This mutual appreciation reinforces Taha's inner peace and makes him attached to his family as much as nature. Finally, going to exotic places opens Taha's eyes to the reality of how big the world is and teaches him that there is always more to learn and give. Taha needs time-off to recharge his energy to go back to human world and be a better effective member in his society.

2.9.4. Paragraph Four (thinking as an insider; viewing the small picture)

- Topic: think inside the box
- Brainstorming: details, box, problem, insider, outsider, live experience, get closer, the small picture vs. the big picture.
- Outline:

I. Introduction.

a. Thesis: Thinking as an insider is as important as thinking of the big picture.

II. Body

a. Supporting idea: maintain details

b. Supporting idea: live the experience

c. Supporting idea: effective solutions in the long run

III. Conclusion.

Paragraph

Thinking of the big picture is always recommended because it helps the individual view the situation as an outsider in order to get the general perspective of a given topic. On the other hand, constantly viewing issues as an outsider is likely to result in focusing on the general features and ignoring the details which are as crucial. Thinking as an insider is as important as thinking of the big picture. By thinking as an insider, the thinker can view the details and always put them in mind when coming up with new strategies. For example, the teacher needs to think as a student when designing the test so that he/she does not make a test that takes longer than class time to be finished by the students. Moreover, it is important for the thinker to live the experience as an insider in order to achieve better results. A teacher of English who gives TOEFL preparation workshops to international students can achieve more effective results if he/she takes the test and tries to get a high score. This reveals points of strength and weaknesses the examinee has and therefore enables the teacher to design courses that better address student's needs to prepare for the test as well as their college work when they start their academic programs. In general, it follows that viewing the insider perspective is as important as viewing it as an outsider.

Exercise 1. Write short paragraphs for each of the following outlines.

1. Topic: camping
- Brainstorming: go with friends, sleep in tent, outdoors, make fire, marshmallow, bugs, dangerous animals, connect with nature, weather, walking, canned food, experience.
- Outline:

I. Introduction.

a. Thesis: Camping is one of the best and enjoyable experiences I have ever had.

II. Body

a. Supporting idea: weather

b. Supporting idea: marshmallow, make fire and sing

c. Supporting idea: connect with nature

III. Conclusion.

2. Topic: music
- Brainstorming: tones, instruments, listening, enjoy, play, sing along, dance, loud, cannot focus, harmony, different world, tell a story, conversation.
- Outline:

I. Introduction.

a. Thesis: As an instrument player and an artist with a musical ear, Husain has a unique relationship with music.

II. Body

a. Supporting idea: bonding with the instrument

b. Supporting idea: tones tell stories

c. Supporting idea: reach out to feelings of others.

III. Conclusion.

Husain talks to music

3. Topic: sleeping early
- Brainstorming: go to bed, enough sleep, midnight, healthy life style, wake up early, more active, lazy, sleepy, yawn, snore, have work done, more punctual.
- Outline:

I. Introduction.

a. Thesis: Going to bed early is important to have a healthy life.

II. Body

a. Supporting idea: enough sleep

b. Supporting idea: wake up early

c. Supporting idea: active at work/school

III. Conclusion.

4. Topic: cooking
- Brainstorming: art, food, desert, burn food, overcook, cut myself, clean, wash dishes, salad, grocery shopping, side dish, light candles, recipes, fruits,
- Outline:

I. Introduction.

a. Thesis: I have a great passion in cooking and I want to make it my future career.

II. Body

a. Supporting idea: my mother's recipes

b. Supporting idea: new recipes

c. Supporting idea: cooking is art

III. Conclusion.

5. Topic: hearing dogs
- Brainstorming: dogs, trained, good friends, allowed in different places, deaf people, assist, alert for sounds, sound recognition, obedience, socialize.
- Outline:

I. Introduction.

a. Thesis: Hearing dogs are special aid assistant dogs which are trained to do certain tasks to individuals with hearing problems.

II. Body

a. Supporting idea: training the dogs

b. Supporting idea: how they do the tasks

c. Supporting idea: accessibility (can they go with their owner anywhere?)

III. Conclusion.

6. Topic: Japan
- Brainstorming: technology, electronics auto, sushi, Fuji, robots, science, investment, big companies, economy, inventions.
- Outline:

I. Introduction.

a. Thesis: Japan is the real definition of industrial revolution in science, electronics and automobile manufactory.

II. Body

a. Supporting idea: science technology

b. Supporting idea: electronic technology

c. Supporting idea: auto technology

III. Conclusion.

————————— ✦ ✦ ✦ ✦ ✦ ✦ —————————

Exercise 2. Read the following sentences then follow the instructions below:

1. Our school soccer team needs more practice before the game.
2. Social media has caused more troubles than communicating in real life.
3. Fruits and vegetables are healthy substitutes to snacks.
4. Film making is becoming a prosperous business in Korea.
5. My mother and I do not have anything in common.
6. The weather tomorrow is not going to be as nice as it is today.
7. Preparation to the graduation party is going to be hard-work and time consuming.
8. I am going to register in the annual city running contest this year.
9. Based on what I see, your kitchen needs serious remodeling.
10. My friend Ali likes to go fishing in winter.

Ali goes fishing

1. Find the topic and the controlling idea in each of these sentences.
2. Make three supporting sentences for each one of them.
3. Rephrase the sentences and make sure you keep the same meaning.

————————— ✦ ✦ ✦ ✦ ✦ —————————

Exercise 3. Decide whether the following topic sentences are too specific (write S) or too general (write G).

1. Education in Spain is compulsory from kindergarten to high school. _____.
2. There are many criteria to consider when applying for classes in a university. _____.
3. Those shoes are tight from the front and do not have a nice color. _____.
4. Your resume must include all the jobs you have had with your recent one on the top of the list. _____.
5. The weather, location, and schools in this city are the major reasons why we relocate here. _____.
6. Community colleges are expanding noticeably in recent years for three major reasons. _____.

——————— ✦✦◆✦✦ ———————

Exercise 4. Fill the table with the missing information:

General Topic	Narrow Topic	Thesis Statement
	Uniforms in high schools	
Technology		Using electronic devices at school can facility learning and make it more enjoyable.
	Parents access child's accounts	
Dishonesty	Plagiarism	

Exercise 5. Write a topic sentence for each of the following paragraphs.

1. .... First, I need to finish writing my book and prepare it for publishing. Second, I must meet with my friend every day in the library to finish the research paper before the deadline. And finally, I have to tutor three high school students for their final test on Math. As you can see, I have a very busy schedule this semester with hardly enough time to finish all of my work.

2. .... It is smaller than the city I used to live in. In addition, everyone is very sociable. Whenever you walk past someone, they always smile at you. Also, the rent is very affordable that I do not need a roommate to share the place with. I will definitely recommend this place for people who want to live a peaceful, happy life.

3. .... I am scared of heights; I cannot go to higher floors in big buildings not to mention being on an airplane! Everybody was sitting quietly, fastened their seat belts and prepared for the flight. I, on the other hand, was nervous and covered in sweat. The flight attendant tried to calm me down because I was very stressed. I closed my eyes and decided to think of good memories to distract myself from my fears. This was my very first time flying on an airplane, and it is definitely my last.

4. .... It is held on October 31 every year. People wear customs and scary make-up. Children wearing customs go around the neighborhood to knock doors and ask for candy by saying 'trick or treat'. Everybody prepares for Halloween and shops for customs online and in stores. Halloween is fun time; it is family time.

5. ....For example, peer pressure can be a big motive for students and employees to persevere and succeed. It is one good way to improve self-esteem and make people believe in their potentials. In some cases, peer pressure results in losing self-confidence and makes the individuals lose hope in themselves because they believe they are worthless. However, it can also make them accept the challenge and decide to prove themselves to themselves and to others. Peer pressure pushes the person to the extremes; it is up to the person to choose which extreme to be pushed towards.

––––––––––––––– ✦✦◆✦✦ –––––––––––––––

Exercise 6. Write a concluding sentence for these paragraphs

1. Subjects such as science and mathematics are not easy to learn or to teach; and therefore, new approaches to teach such subjects more effectively are always developed. STEM education is an interdisciplinary approach used to provide new more effective teaching methods to teach the four disciplines of Science, Technology, Engineering and Math together rather than teaching them separately as discrete subjects. This method of teaching is growing throughout the United Sates schools because it deals with all aspects in our lives. As a result, STEM-based curriculum includes authentic situations derived from real life in order to help the students comprehend these subjects. This teaching method is important today in the world of knowledge-base economy and globalization. ....

2. I have had no idea that travelling requires a lot of planning. First, I need to contact a travel agency to find a tourist guide who can speak my language. Second, I need to book flight tickets and make hotel reservations. Then I have to make sure I keep my luggage load within the limited weight. After that, I need to bring enough cash with me because some purchases cannot be made with my card or I have to pay extra if I use a card. And finally, I have to read about the country I'm visiting in order to know what to prepare for, what to expect, and the places to visit. ....

3. Applying for a college program requires potential students to take many steps. First, they need to choose the major that is appropriate for their future academic and professional careers. They also need to consider funding options by either applying for a scholarship or contacting the financial aid office for help. Moreover, the students need to get in touch with an academic advisor to help them choose what classes to enroll in for each semester. ....

4. In order to maintain good health, I need to have a healthy life style. First of all, it is important that I eat healthy food. Instead of completely deprive myself from sugary and carbohydrate products, I eat fewer portions of them with more amounts of vegetables and fruits. Additionally, I drink water and exercise more often on a daily basis. Lastly, I keep positive attitude all the time and surround myself in an environment that does not produce negative energy. ....

5. There are many factors to consider when you decide to buy a smart phone. One important factor is to learn more about operating systems that smart phones have and the differences between them. For example, you need to know the differences between iOS and Android. Another factor to consider is choosing the phone that has the features that mostly appeal to you. Most of popular applications such as Google, Apple Music and Maps are available in all operating systems. However, some other applications, e.g. Facetime, and iMessage are only provided for the company's platform. And finally, you need to decide the price range based on your budget. Accessories such as the case and the headset and an extra charger should be included in the budget. ....

44

Exercise 7. Fill in the table with two different controlling ideas for each topic.

Topic	Controlling Idea 1	Controlling Idea 2
1. Winter		
2. Having a pet cat		
3. Evening classes		
4. Vegetable pizza		
5. Buying used furniture		

Exercise 8. Write a short paragraph for each of the following outlines

1. Topic: Think inside the box
- Brainstorming: old school, traditional ways, profound, tested and guaranteed, taking risk, danger, ineffective, go with the flow, break tradition.
- Outline:

I. Introduction.

a. Thesis: Thinking inside the box is required alongside with thinking outside of it.

II. Body

a. Supporting idea: traditional (e.g. return of midwifery practice, use the fireplace instead of the heater)

b. Supporting idea: guaranteed results

c. Supporting idea: not taking risks

III. Conclusion.

2. Topic: Different shades of grey
- Brainstorming: yes, no, black grey, white, certain extent, agree and disagree, take the best option, the other perspective, explore other reasons.
- Outline:

I. Introduction.

a. Thesis: It is not black or white anymore, it is different shades of grey

II. Body

    a. Supporting idea: selection

    b. Supporting idea: different appropriate things for different situations

    c. Supporting idea: flexibility

III. Conclusion.

    3. Topic: addiction to the internet

    - Brainstorming: internet, addiction, long hours, distraction, not functional,
    - Outline:

I. Introduction.

    a. Thesis: Walid sees some advantages to getting addicted to the internet

II. Body

    a. Supporting idea: learn about new things regularly

    b. Supporting idea: become cognitively skillful at games

    c. Supporting idea: make money (e.g. blogger, youtuber).

III. Conclusion.

Walid sees some advantages to getting addicted to the internet

Chapter Three

Paragraph Extension

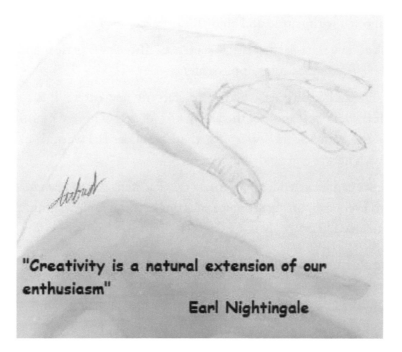

"Creativity is a natural extension of our enthusiasm"

Earl Nightingale

As covered in the previous chapter, the supporting sentences in the paragraph constitute the body part. Although the details in these sentences are limited to the controlling idea in the topic sentence, they can be discussed in more details in sub-sequencing sentences. This means that a small paragraph can be extended into a longer essay. This chapter explains the strategies to do that.

3.1. How to Extend a Short Paragraph into an Essay

The best strategy to do this is to answer one or more of the following questions: who, where, when, which, what, and how. Take a look at this sentence:

This city is perfect and can be the place where I can start my new career.

The information in this sentence can be elaborated by giving more details to it. For example, the sentence contains two keywords that call for extra explanation. The first word is the adjective 'perfect'; this adjective makes the reader wonder *why* this city in particular is perfect for the writer. As a result, we can add one sentence that explains why this city is seen to be perfect by the writer. Here is an example:

It is a small city that has a big lake and nice weather.

The second keyword is 'career'. The writer needs to explain *how* these city's characteristics are connected to his/her career. The writer can provide more details to this word by explaining how staying in this city can help with their career. For example:

My yoga students can enjoy the sound of the water near the lake under the warmth of sunshine.

Interestingly, we can still find new key words in the new two sentences and create more sentences. Here is an example of the first extended sentence:

It is a small city that has a big lake and nice weather. It is warm here most of the year with wonderful breezy mornings in the summer.

And here is an example of the second extended sentence:

My yoga students can enjoy the sound of the water near the lake under the warmth of sunshine. This enables them to get connected with nature and enjoy inner peace.

Now let's take a look at how the very first single sentence "This city is perfect and can be the place where I can start my new career"; is extended to multiple sentences:

This city is perfect and can be the place where I can start my new career. It is a small city that has a big lake and nice weather. It is warm here most of the year with wonderful breezy mornings in the summer. My yoga students can enjoy the sound of the water near the lake under the warmth of sunshine. This enables them to get connected with nature and enjoy inner peace.

As shown, one sentence can be extended into many other sentences and become a separate paragraph. If this strategy is used with every supporting sentence in a single- paragraph writing, this paragraph becomes a longer essay. This is explained below.

3.2. Extending One Paragraph into an Essay

In this paragraph, we will add more information to each supporting sentence in order to turn the paragraph into a longer essay.

I have decided to improve my financial status. My salary only covers the rent and the bills. Moreover, I have to pay for grocery shopping, and food for my dog. Finally, there is health insurance that I need to pay for. As a result, I see the need to find another source of income to help me earn more money.

This short paragraph contains many pieces of information that can be elaborated in new sentences. Let's first break it down into the three major components.

Introduction: I have decided to improve my financial status.

Body: My salary only covers the rent and the bills. Moreover, I have to pay for grocery shopping, and food for my dog. Finally, there is health insurance that I need to pay for.

Conclusion: As a result, I see the need to find another source of income to help me earn more money.

Now we can add more sentences to each part. We will start with the introduction.

3. 2.1. Introduction

I have decided to improve my financial status.

This sentence functions as a topic sentence in the paragraph. Therefore, it can be preceded by an attention getter. Here is an example:

Life is always a demanding nonstop process

This works as a good attention getter because it is a general statement that motivates the reader to read more. However, the ideas should be developed gradually; i.e., we cannot talk about money immediately after talking about life. The topic needs to move slowly from life to money, and this process takes at least a couple of sentences. For example,

Life is always a demanding nonstop process. In other words, once one thing is accomplished, a new one emerges. In addition, the same demand is likely to occur again after it is met and keeps coming over and over. These demands are mostly met via financial mean; in that, they need money in order to be accomplished appropriately and fully. I, as an individual, have many demands that require money to be fulfilled. As a result, I have decided to improve my financial status.

As shown, the sentences move from talking about life demands to the writer's own demands and his/her need for money to meet these demands. In this case, the introductory paragraph is ready. The next step is to expand every supporting sentence into a separate paragraph in order to form the body paragraphs.

3.2.2. Body

The first supporting sentence is: My salary only covers the rent and the bills.

We can add more details to this sentence and talk more about the salary, the rent, and the bills. First we start with a sentence about the salary. As understood from the topic sentence, the salary is not big; therefore, we can talk about the effort put in the job compared with the financial outcome. For example:

My salary is not much. I have been a very hard-working person but I still cannot get a raise.

More details can be added to emphasize the difficulty of getting a better solution for the job. Here is one suggestion:

Moreover, I have failed to find another part-time job as an additional source of income

Two sentences are added about the job. We still need to elaborate on the rent and the bills. We can give a description of the place and the reason(s) why it is chosen, and we provide sentences about the things that we pay bills for. For instance, we can say:

I live in a one-bedroom apartment in a quiet and safe neighborhood; as a result, the rent is considerably high. I do not have a car; therefore I have chosen this place because it is close to where I work so that I can ride my bike. My salary is not much. I have been a very hard-working person but I still cannot get a raise. Moreover, I have failed to find another part-time job as an additional source of income. In addition, the rent does not include utilities, so I have to be careful in consuming gas and electricity. I get higher bills in the winter because I use the heater a lot. Although the internet and the phone bills are reasonably affordable, they still take a considerable amount of my paycheck.

One more sentence that needs to be added to this paragraph is the one that connects it to the next paragraph. Based on the supporting sentences of the original paragraph, the next idea under discussion is paying for grocery shopping and food for the dog. Accordingly, we need a transitional sentence that takes the essay from talking about paying the bills to talking about buying food. Here is an example:

With all these payments I make for the rent and the bills, I do not have much left for food shopping.

This finishes our first body paragraph and takes us to the second one. This is the second supporting sentence:

I have to pay for grocery shopping, and food for my dog.

More sentences can be added to each part of this sentence: grocery shopping and dog food. In this case, we end up with sentences like these:

I am careful to have a healthy diet. Therefore, I need to buy lots of fruits and vegetables in addition to dairy products. Also, I need to have cereal, eggs, and pasta. These products are costly and they are constantly consumed. As a result, I have to buy a large amount at least twice every ten days. This is the case with the dog food as well; I have to buy a large amount of it in order to make sure I never run out of it. Dog food is the same as our food, it has different brands and flavors, and dogs, just like humans, have specific food preferences too.

As we did with the second paragraph in the body part, we need to end this paragraph with a sentence that connects it to the next one. Since the next supporting sentence is: *there is health insurance*, here is a suggestion for a last sentence to the second body paragraph:

Despite the fact that I need to spend money on food, this is nothing compared to the payments I have to make for my health insurance.

Now that we have the second body paragraph complete, we have one last paragraph in the body section. This paragraph discusses tuition fees and health insurance. Therefore, we need sentences for that. For example:

Finally, there is health insurance that I need to pay for. I have to pay for the regular check –ups every six months. Also, my insurance does not cover dental care so I am responsible for my dental bills. Likewise, I need to pay for my vision check-ups every three months. In addition, I have to be ready for emergencies in case I suddenly get sick and need to go to the walk-in clinic.

3.2.3. Conclusion

The last body paragraph does not need to end with a sentence that connects it to the next paragraph. The reason is the next paragraph is the conclusion so it follows the 'specific to general' pattern. It is, in a way, the introduction reversed. First let's revise the concluding sentence in the original paragraph:

As a result, I see the need to find another source of income to help me earn more money.

This sentence can be used to start the concluding paragraph because it is specific to the main idea. Following this sentence, more general sentences can be added to give the complete ending of the essay. For example:

As a result, I see the need to find another source of income to help me earn more money. Therefore, improving ourselves financially should become part of our life style in order to be able to deal with the daily demands we go through. Being financially independent helps us become more responsible and more ready to live in this world. This makes seeking better ways to improve our financials very crucial to handle the challenging life we go through.

Now we have the whole essay ready.

Life is always a demanding nonstop process. In other words, once one thing is accomplished, another one emerges. In addition, the same demand is likely to occur again after it is met and keeps coming over and over. These demands are mostly met via financial means, in that they need money to be accomplished appropriately and fully. I as an individual have many demands that require money to be fulfilled. As a result, I have decided to improve my financial status.

I live in a one-bedroom apartment in a quiet and safe neighborhood; as a result, the rent is considerably high. I do not have a car; therefore I have chosen a place that is close to where I work so that I can ride my bike. My salary is not much. I have been a very hard-working person but I still cannot get a raise. Moreover, I have failed to find another part-time job as an additional source of income. In addition, the rent does not include utilities, so I have to be careful in consuming gas and electricity. I get higher bills in the winter because I use the heater a lot. Although the internet and the phone bills are reasonably affordable, they still take a considerable amount of my paycheck.

I am careful to have a healthy diet. Therefore, I need to buy lots of fruits and vegetables in addition to dairy products. Also, I need to have cereal, eggs, and pasta. These products are costly and they are constantly consumed. As a result, I have to buy a large amount at least twice every ten days. This is the case with the dog food as well; I have to buy a large amount of it in order to make sure I never run out of it. Dog food is the same as our food, it has different brands and flavors, and dogs, just like humans, have specific food preferences too. Despite the fact that I need to spend money on food, this is nothing compared to the payments I have to make for my tuition and health insurance.

Finally, there is health insurance that I need to pay for. I have to pay for the regular check –ups every six months. Also, my insurance does not cover dental care so I am responsible for my dental bills. Likewise, I need to pay for my vision check-ups every three months. In addition, I have to be ready for emergencies in case I suddenly get sick and need to go to the walk-in clinic.

As a result, I see the need to find another source of income to help me earn more money. Therefore, improving ourselves financially should become part of our life style in order to be able to deal with the daily demands we go through. Being financially independent helps us become more responsible and more ready to live in this world. This makes seeking better ways to improve our financials very crucial to handle the challenging life we go through.

3.3. Sample Essay 1

Here is an example of a short paragraph turned into an essay.

Paragraph

My name is Meftah, I am 28 years old. I have always wanted to graduate from the School of Medicine and become an orthopedic sergeant. Unfortunately, in my fourth year of college, I had an accident that has left me on a wheel-chair ever since. As a result, I have given up my dream to become an orthopedic sergeant and decide to major either in internal medicine or dermatology as these two majors do not require a lot of physical movement. The decision is not easy but I have to not give up on my dream to become a doctor.

Meftah, a student in the School of Medicine

Essay

My name is Meftah, and I am 28 years old. Ever since I was a teenager, I have always wanted to graduate from the School of Medicine and become an orthopedic sergeant. The reason for choosing this specialty is that it is highly demanded and is always a prolific field for research. Moreover, it provides the chance to develop my knowledge and get myself updated with recent medicine developments in this field. For all these reasons, I was very determined and studied hard in high school in order to get the GPA required for admission to the School of Medicine. However, things did not go as desired and I had to reconsider my dream due to my new health condition that required me to find more appealing alternatives.

As a medical student, I have started college with high hopes and enthusiasm and was a hard-working student until I got to fourth year. Unfortunately, in my fourth year of college, I had an accident that left me on a wheelchair and this hindered me from pursuing the major of my dreams. As a result, I gave up my dream to become an orthopedic sergeant and decided to major either in internal medicine or dermatology as these two majors do not require a lot of physical movement. Moreover, these majors help me keep updated and learn more about new advancements in these fields. In addition, I have a good chance with a future job since these two majors are among the ones required in many hospitals and clinics.

I am highly determined to fulfilling my dreams. It is my belief that seeking alternatives will always make me happy and satisfied. I also believe that hard work always pays off at the end, and that good results wipe off memories of hardship. Although the decision of changing my major is challenging as it entails shifting all my future plans to a different direction, I know I should never give up on my dream to become a successful doctor.

3.4. Sample Essay 2

Here is another example of paragraph extension.

Paragraph

Suburban Sprawl is the expansion of population in areas away from the city. Although more people are in favor of living in the suburbs, some still believe that living in the suburbs can have disadvantages. For starters, suburban areas are characterized by having larger houses, better roads, less traffic, and better school districts. On the other hand, people who live in the suburbs are far away from everything; e.g. they have to drive to work, school, and grocery stores. Moreover, the spread of population in the suburbs can have negative impact on the natural environment. Living in the suburbs can be quieter than living in the city; however, residents need to have a car for transportation between the suburb and the city.

Essay

Suburban Sprawl can be defined as the expansion of human population in areas away from the urban cities. Suburban areas are also referred to as urban suburbs because more citizens have become interested in living in the suburbs instead of other metropolitan regions. Although more people are in favor of living in the suburbs because they believe it has many benefits, some still believe that living in the suburbs can have disadvantages.

One advantage of living in the suburbs is that the houses are more spacious than the houses and apartments in the city. Families can have separate bedrooms for their children, and this provides more privacy for them. Also, big houses are more convenient for parties and other social gatherings. Furthermore, the roads in the suburbs are wide and new. They are easy to drive on with automobiles and bicycles, and they are not crowded as much as the city. Lastly, schools in suburban districts are safe and better equipped with staff, updated textbooks and supplies. Nevertheless, despite these positive features, living in urban suburbs is not as convenient as it sounds.

Residents of the suburbs are far away from everything; e.g. they have to drive to work, school, and grocery stores. This can be problematic in inclement weather when it rains or snows. In addition, the long drive is likely to put pressure on the residents when they attempt to leave early for their appointments. Finally, the spread of population in the suburbs can have negative impact on the natural environment. More trees are cut to make space for new buildings. Also, the long distance to work, school, and recreational areas calls for the demand to bring these destinations closer to the residential areas in the suburbs. This increases the likelihood of pollution caused by factories and cars.

As living in the suburb can provide more space and socialization than living in the city, the increasing demand to live in the suburb is likely to bring different aspects of the city to it. Consequently, the suburb can become a city by time as more people move to live in it and bring their city favorites with them.

3.5. Sample Essay 3

Paragraph

A social force is an action and/ or reaction that is based on a generally perceived consensus of the nature of social roles and the behaviors expected to be done in different situations. Contrary to traditional beliefs that human behavior is arbitrary and random, such actions are said to determine the basic drives and motivations that form social relationships and cultural associations. It follows that changes are likely to occur in human behavior based on the nature of the stimulus that makes it take place. There are two major social forces that determine the nature of human behavior. The first one is perception; i.e., stereotypical expectations about different social status and the roles played by different individuals. The second is related to the individual's personality and current state of mind in the given situation. Social forces frame human behavior and their relationships with each other as well as the society. Although they are universal, social forces are culture-specific in that they are embraced differently from one culture to another.

Essay

A social force is an action and/ or reaction that is based on a generally perceived consensus of the nature of social roles of individuals in the society and the behaviors expected to be done in different complex situations. In other words, certain situations demand specific kinds of reactions that are imposed upon the individual by social forces. Contrary to traditional beliefs that human behavior is arbitrary and random, such actions are said to determine the basic drives and motivations that form social relationships and cultural associations. It follows that changes are likely to occur in human behavior based on the nature of the stimulus that makes the action take place. There are two major social forces that determine the nature of human behavior; namely perception and personality.

Perception is associated with stereotypical expectations about different social status and the roles played by different individuals. For example, the roles of power and solidarity are naturally performed by individuals such as parents, police officers, sports trainers, chef surgeons, etc. Interestingly, these roles are automatically played in unrealistic situations such as role plays and research studies. A good example of this behavior is the famous 70s Zimbardo Prison Situation study conducted on a group of Stanford University students. The experiment included dividing the students into two groups; one group was instructed to play the role of a prisoner, the other group was given the role of a prison guard. The prisoners went through the real prison process of arresting, strip search, and wearing prison uniform. Likewise, the guards were given uniforms, clubs and whistles. The findings reveal that the students who were characterized prior to the study as being emotionally stable and assigned the guard roles became aggressive, brutal and sadistic; i.e. the role they played triggered the status of power and solidarity those students experienced. Similarly, emotionally stable students in the prisoner group displayed passive attitude and surrendered to the guards' commands. Although the two groups were aware that this was not a real situation, they still acted according to background knowledge on the basis of social roles expected from each individual. In other words, actions and attitudes are selected according to social status of people involved in the given situation.

The second social force that affects human behavior is related to the individual's personality and current state of mind in a specific situation. The pressure co-workers undergo has an impact on their relationships with each other in both positive and negative ways. For example, there are cases in which surgeons in the ER scream at each other due to the pressure they are exposed to as they try to save lives. In such situations, different kinds of actions and reactions are likely to emerge; an intern may not do what their resident tells them to do for one reason or another. However, the situation is different when those doctors are in a less stressful situation. Likewise, a middle -school girl may give her father specific and direct instructions not to cheer loudly for her during her soccer game because this embarrasses her in front of her friends. Fathers in such situations are likely to listen and agree despite their social status which puts them in the position of power and solidarity in the household. Human behavior, though systematic to general rules, is significantly contextual and goes under certain changes demanded to handle the situation in hand.

Social forces frame human behavior and their relationships with each other as well as the society. Although they are universal, social forces are culture-specific in that they are embraced differently from one culture to another. Every situation is expected to be handled in certain ways determined by the social status of the individuals involved and the nature of the situation itself.

Change the following short paragraphs into longer essays

1. The poet Salah intends to publish his first book that contains his new collection of poems in Arabic. He contacts the printing house to make appropriate arrangements. He is told to reedit some poems due to occasional typos that occur in the poems. As a result, Salah decides to seek help from a professor of Arabic in the university to help him correct grammar and spelling mistakes. During their meetings, Salah learns a lot from the professor as they work together in the poems. The professor suggests that Salah enrolls in the writing center workshop in the university in order to improve the linguistic structure of his poems. Accordingly, Salah decides to enroll in the workshop to learn more about the complicated grammar of Arabic.

Poet Salah intends to publish his poem collection

2. Contrary to the widely spread belief that material achievement is the source of happiness, it is stated that social relationships are the key factor to real happiness. Individuals who think of themselves as happy people are said to be in healthful engagement with their families and friends. This is likely to lead to better feelings towards school, work and life in general. Social environment can function as a good source of inspiration to better feelings about one's self.

3. I have always wanted to go camping because I hear a lot of stories about it. Last weekend, I went camping with friends in order to experience one of these stories in person. Despite my expectations, the camping trip I took was bad and boring. First of all, it was cold and cloudy most of the time. We could not make fire because of the heavy rain. Moreover, I could not sleep because I kept hearing the howling of wolves and other scary sounds of wild animals. In addition, we had to walk long hours to find a good spot to set the tents. I do not like long walks especially on muddy ground. To sum up, camping is not my cup of tea.

4. We always see people announce New Year resolutions by the end or beginning of every year. A New Year resolution is a decision made by an individual to either make new achievements or improve already existing ones. Resolutions are made about many things from keeping the bedroom clean to learning a new language or getting an academic scholarship or graduating, etc. Although not everybody adheres to the resolutions they make, many people take these resolutions seriously and make new ones every year.

5. Antarctica is a very cold continent on the South Pole of the planet. This continent is not a good habitat for humans and most other creatures. The temperature there drops to as low as 100° F degrees below zero or even lower than that. There are some polar animals that live in Antarctica such as penguins and whales. The air in Antarctica is dry, and the wind is strong there. Although some scientists stay temporarily in Antarctica to work on their scientific research, it is never home for any human.

6. Although music is enjoyable all over the world, my grandmother is an exception. My grandmother dislikes music. Due to her hearing problems, my grandmother says that music is loud and gives her a headache. She refuses to stay in the house when we have a party so we take her to her friend to spend the time there until the party is over. Also, she does not allow us to play music after 9:00 p.m. unless we use headsets because she wants to sleep quietly and peacefully. My grandmother thinks that music does not help her focus on the activities she loves to do such as gardening and painting. She says these activities require complete silence! Although music is technically a universal language, people who do not desire to listen to it do exist.

7. An endangered species can be defined as a one population of creatures that encounter the risk of becoming extinct. Reasons for the potential extinction of some creatures vary. Hunting is a one leading reason to extinction. Another reason is natural disasters and the destruction of natural habitats of these creatures. A third reason can be attributed to the bad services provided to protect these creatures. More work should be done to provide better protecting conditions to these species.

8. A ban on swimming too close to Dolphins off the coast of Hawaii has been proposed by Hawaiian authorities. There has been an overload pressure put on the dolphins by tourists who sail near those creatures and snorkel with them. This decision is justified by the fact that dolphins tend to be active at night, and sleep during the day. Therefore, swimming near them can disturb their comfort and that can negatively affect their health and fitness. It is said that the ban which prohibits swimming with the dolphins in a distances not closer than 50 meters does not have undesired impact on tourism in Hawaii.

9. Having future goals helps planning for both current and upcoming times, and encourages preparing for prosperous productive careers. Landon is a student in the university majoring in law enforcement. He believes that hard-work, no matter how exhausting and time-consuming, always pays-off eventually. He enjoys practicing his favorite sports; archery and skiing. Constant practice has made Landon a skillful archer who wins many archery competitions in addition to achievement recognitions. Moreover, he always goes skiing in winter with his friends to improve his skiing ability while having fun with his friends. In addition to keeping himself athletically fit, Landon plans to become a dedicated police officer and desires to have a private business in the future. There is no end to how far Landon goes with his plans and future goals because he believes that the sky is the limit.

Landon likes to practice archery

10. Contrary to traditional beliefs that human actions are decided based on personal choices, it is proved that our actions are determined in relation to an ethical framework that sets the boundaries to freedom of choice. These boundaries put into consideration factors such as religion, politics, and culture in addition to common sense among others which are used to classify right and wrong choices in ethical decisions. Although many decisions are made on good intentions to adhere to ethical rules, unethical choices are still made. The argument here is whether planning to maintain ethical standard can justify making harmful decisions; this conflict in decision making is referred to as ethical dilemma. Establishing ethical standards is said to be cultural-specific, in that what is considered to be ethical in one culture is not always the same in another culture. Ethical dilemma can emerge in a situation in

which the individual needs to choose between two hard decisions; a situation in which the choice that causes less harm to ethical standards is likely to be chosen. However, such a choice does not always appeal to the person in that it is not an ethical decision. For example, is it acceptable to scarify the life of one person to save other five people? In other words, do good intentions justify wrong deeds? It follows that in some cases, adhering to ethical standards can very likely result in costly consequences that may not be related to ethics.

Chapter 4

Writing a Summary

" It is not the beauty of a building
you should look at; its the
construction of teh foundation that
will stand the test of time"
David Allan Coe

Developing the skill to summarize is required in academic writing. When students work on their essays, they need to read other works about the targeted topic. This calls for writing strategies such as paraphrasing, quoting, and summarizing. Furthermore, summarizing is needed when writing annotated bibliographies, abstracts, and proposals. It follows that improving the skills to summarize is crucial for better academic writing.

When summarizing, it is important to focus on recapping the main idea and primary supporting ideas in a brief form rather than rewriting details. In other words, the purpose of summarizing is to focus on the big picture of the given topic and to present it in a concise manner. Generally speaking, the characteristics of a good summary include the following:

- Synthesize the author's main idea and key relevant elements.
- Provide the information without quotations.
- Paraphrase (use you own words).
- Present the topic objectively; i.e., avoid making personal judgments.
- The summary does not have to be very short, but it is shorter than the original text (approximately one-third of the original text).
- Include citation when possible.

Regarding the last point (citation), in some cases such information is not provided either because it is not available, or because it is not applicable, or for other possible reasons. Nevertheless, citation is crucially important in academic writing, and students must always do it whenever they can.

Some may ask: what is the difference between paraphrasing and summarizing? The answer is that paraphrasing can be as long as the original text, sometimes even longer when replacing single words with phrases. On the other hand, the most important characteristic of summarizing is to make it shorter than the original text. While summarizing includes paraphrasing, the process of paraphrasing conveys the same message with no aim to summarize.

4.1. How to Summarize

Here are the steps to follow when summarizing:

1. Read the material you intend to summarize very carefully.
2. Identify the main idea in the text (the thesis).
3. Indentify the supporting ideas (topic sentences).
4. Paraphrase the main idea and the supporting points.
5. Compare your sentences to the original ones to make sure you have covered the meaning thoroughly.
6. Make sure NOT to add extra information on your own.
7. If needed, rewrite your own sentences and use conjunctions and transition words to connect all the ideas.

After discussing how to paraphrase single sentences in chapter 1, we now move to explain how to summarize paragraphs and essays.

4.2. Summarizing a paragraph

Based on the outline used to write single paragraphs, the main idea is generally located at the beginning of the paragraph, though not necessarily the very first sentence. Below are some examples of how to summarize a paragraph.

4.2.1. Summarizing a Paragraph (example one)

Paragraph

The increasingly growing number of working married couples puts these families into possibilities of opportunities and challenges. A second financial resource provides alternatives for better financial and social life. Moreover, working ladies feel more independent, self-fulfilled, and capable of living up to their expectations. Also, working parents set a good example to their children and indirectly teach them the value of work. All of this works to strengthen the bonds between the couple, gives them a better healthy life and marriage, and brings the parents closer to their children. However, along with these advantages, families with working parents face challenges that cause stress. One challenge is time conflict between work and family. There is a chance dinner table may miss one of the parents in some days. There is also the possibility that a working parent may need to attend a conference that requires them to travel. Furthermore, working parents may not find it easy to have full-time jobs and take care of children at a young age and/or teenage kids who demand constant attention and care. Although working parents can provide better financial and social life to their family, this goal is not achieved easily and can be stressful to those parents and their families.

Summary

The first step to summarizing is to read the paragraph carefully. Then comes the next step; identifying the main idea. The main idea is provided in the first sentence which functions as the topic sentence of the paragraph. The topic is about working parents, the controlling idea is the advantages and disadvantages of having working parents in the family. The rest of the paragraph presents examples of each case. Therefore, the topic sentence can be paraphrased into the following sentence:

There are advantages and disadvantages of having working parents in a family.

Now we rephrase the key points; i.e., the advantages and disadvantages. We will start with the advantages:

- Working couples provide higher income to the family.
- It makes wives become more independent.
- It teaches children that work is important.
- And here are the disadvantages:
- It causes time conflict.
- A parent may have to travel.
- Hard to spend more time with children.

The concluding sentence in the paragraph restates the main idea. It can be paraphrased as follows:

In order for working parents to achieve good family relationships and better financial status, they face challenges that can be stressful.

Now all we need is to put these sentences together and make the necessary adjustments. For example, we may need to rearrange the ideas and join the sentences with appropriate conjunctions and transitions. The following is one suggestion of a summary to the paragraph:

There are advantages and disadvantages of having working parents in a family. One advantage is that working couples provide higher income to the family. Another advantage is that having a job makes wives become more independent. Also, it teaches children that work is important. However, working parents may face the challenge of time conflict, may have to travel and stay away from their family and it can be hard to spend more time with children. In order for working parents to achieve good family relationships and better financial status, they face challenges that can be stressful.

As explained at the beginning of the chapter, the summary does not have to be short, but it is relatively shorter than the original text.

4.2.2. Summarizing a paragraph (example two)

Paragraph

As former and/or current students, we have all had times in which we daze off in class. We all know it happens but we have no idea why it does. Students tend to be unfocused in class for many different reasons. One reason is the lack of recreational time. According to research, students who get a recess period that is 45 minutes long show significant improvement in their grades. Long recess helps students recharge their energy after attending classes that require students to focus attentively for at least 45 minutes for each class. Another reason that is attributed to students' lethargy in class is not getting enough physical activities for a long time. Students go to school from about 8:00 a.m. to 3:30 p.m. from kindergarten until high school. These are 16 years of the students' youth spent mostly sitting in classroom chairs. Young students are full of energy and need to vent it in a healthy way. Exercising enables students to maintain a healthy and balanced life that is required to focus in class. As can be seen, taking a break and exercising more can be of great assistance to students to stay focused and concentrate in class.

Summary

After reading the paragraph, the topic sentence can be easily spotted:

Students tend to be unfocused in class for many different reasons.

A paraphrased sentence to the topic sentence can look like the following:

There are reasons why students fail to concentrate in class.

The next step is to identify the reasons; the paragraph gives two of them:

- Students do not get long recess time.
- Students do not exercise enough.

Finally, we work on the concluding sentence:

As can be seen, taking a break and exercising more can be of great assistance to students to stay focused and concentrate in class.

This sentence is paraphrased as follows:

Longer breaks and frequent exercising are required to help students become more attentive in class.
Here is a summary of the paragraph:

There are reasons why students fail to concentrate in class. One reason is that students do not get enough recess time to help them stay alert in class. Another reason is that students do not exercise enough to focus during class. Longer breaks and frequent exercising are required to help students become more attentive in class.

4.2.3. Summarizing a Paragraph (example three)

In this example, the summary is given immediately after the paragraph is presented.

Paragraph

Choosing a major in college is a serious issue for Shelby because she is concerned that she will be locked in the major she chooses for the rest of her life. Shelby knows that she needs to use reliable resources to decide what major to study in college. The first step she takes is to seek help from current students in college. She contacts a cousin who is in her second semester in the university. The cousin suggests that Shelby should first think of the things she likes to do most of all. After that, Shelby should focus on what she wants her career to be in the future, and the earning potential she wants to achieve. According to her cousin, all these factors are helpful in choosing a good major that serves the student's current and future demands. After careful thinking,

Shelby figures out that she wants to major in chemistry. She has loved chemistry since she was a child and has always had good grades in it. Also, she knows that working in a research center pays pretty decently and can be an excellent future career. Shelby has made her decision by following a good strategy that has helped her decide on a college major.

Shelby wants to major in chemistry

Summary

Shelby decides to seek help to decide what major to choose in college. She asks her cousin who is a college student for advice. The cousin suggests that Shelby thinks of what she likes to do, her future career, and the income she desires to make. Shelby follows these steps and decides to major in chemistry. Shelby chooses a college major wisely because she has consulted for advice.

Next, the discussion focuses on explaining how to summarize essays.

4.3. Summarizing an Essay

Summarizing an essay is not very different from summarizing a single paragraph. In essays, key points in each paragraph are summarized separately, and then they are put together in one single paragraph with the necessary changes made. Changes include rephrasing sentences and connecting them with different transition words. Below is the first essay example.

4.3.1. Summarizing an Essay (example one)

Essay

The business of advertising all kinds of products is everywhere today and is constantly expanding. Different ways to deliver these advertisements are employed, including TV radio stations, internet websites, print and billboards. It is very likely that TV is the most popular way to advertise since it is widely watched by everybody. Posting advertisements on the internet is also highly recommended because it is most specifically used by young population who constitute a perfect marketing target. Advertisement designers aim at making the advertisements as unique and distinguished as possible; therefore, they employ strategies that can deeply get into the audience emotions. For example, we are all familiar with famous Flo, the Progressive Insurance commercial girl who appears in this company's advertisements on TV. Flo has become an icon to that company and a major reason for the huge success of advertisements for their auto insurance. Indeed Progressive Insurance Company has gained success in using a strategy in their commercial advertisements through the audience feelings; this strategy is referred to as emotional appeal.

In the emotional appeal, the advertisement is produced in a way that directly targets the audience emotions, and gradually makes its way to their subconscious thoughts. As a result, this company is the first to come to the customer's heads when they decide to have auto insurance. This strategy significantly works with customers who belong to minor and/ or vulnerable populations that appreciate direct recognition. One example of emotional appeals used by Progressive Company in advertisement is the association of elements based on background stereotypical perspectives. In one of their advertisements, Flo talks about how she likes riding her little pink pony that she puts in the roundabout with other kinds of automobiles. This particular advertisement reflects two background associations; the first is the reference to the color pink that is known to be liked by girls, and the second is the little pony that girls find cute and adorable. This advertisement targets a specific audience; namely ladies, in order to make them more interested in getting this company's auto insurance because they get the feeling that it fulfills their natural needs and affiliations.

Another example that shows how emotional appeals are applied in advertisements for Progressive Company is the one in which two young gentlemen customers express interest into purchasing the affordable insurance the company provides. One guy states that by getting this auto insurance, he will be able to buy his watch back from the other gentleman. It is said that this advertisement addresses individuals of homosexual orientation because it presents insinuations that reinforce our background knowledge of how a homosexual couple is likely to behave. One example of these insinuations that influence judgment of being homosexual is their appearance such as their hair style and the color of their clothes. Moreover, the very narrow personal space between the two guys and the way they look at each other confirm the previously stated assumption.

Although this kind of advertisement may attract a large audience, it is likely to be criticized by many others who may get triggered by possible indignation and discontent that such an advertisement may bring. However, since the purpose of the advertisement is to get the audience attention, both feelings can positively serve this purpose because either group of audience will be thinking of this advertisement especially when the need to have auto insurance comes up. The industry of advertisement is huge and widely spread all over the world because it plays a major role in the customer's subconscious thoughts and can direct them to the products of a certain company over the others and blind them from its possible deprivations.

Based on the summary steps given above, the first thing to do is to read this essay carefully. By reading the last sentence of the introductory paragraph (the thesis), it is understood that the topic is about advertisements produced by Progressive Auto Insurance Company. The controlling idea is focused on a specific type of advertisement; namely, the emotional appeal.

The introductory paragraph starts by presenting general facts about the industry of advertisement and narrows down to advertisement strategies applied in Progressive Company, until lastly the topic specifically addresses the emotional appeals used in this company's advertisements. In other words, the topic is advertisement in Progressive Company, and the controlling idea is the use of emotional appeals in advertisement to promote for their insurance.

Now that we have the main idea rephrased, we can move to the next step which is to avoid adding information of our own. This does not mean not adding words and phrases that do not exist in the paragraph; rather, it means not to add ideas that are not provided in the original text.

Based on this discussion, the summary of the whole introductory paragraph can be provided as the following:

The advertisement industry is growing and developing every day. One example is the emotional appeal strategy of advertisement that is used by Progressive Company to promote for their auto insurance.

As can be seen, this sentence does not include the information provided in the original paragraph that discusses the different media of advertisement. The reason is that this kind of information is considered details that, although related to the topic, are not stated in the summary in which only the main idea and key points are required. Moreover, the summarized sentence includes the transition phrase *one example* which is not already mentioned in the original text. It is taken that transition words and/or conjunctions can be added in the summary provided that they do not change the main idea and the general message of the paragraph.

The first example of the emotional appeal is the use of the pink pony by the progressive girls Flo. The main idea of this paragraph is to discuss the fact that this commercial touches upon feelings of female audience and gives them the motivation to purchase the insurance. Likewise, the second body paragraph also targets a specific audience (homosexual couples) by focusing on the influence of the advertisement on this population's feelings and make it more appealing to them than other insurance companies. Accordingly, the following summary is one example of how the two body paragraphs can be summarized:

In one of their advertisements, Progressive Company targets the emotions of ladies by showing how their famous commercial girl Flo is obsessed with riding a pink pony. Similarly, the homosexual population is targeted in the Company's other advertisement in which a homosexual couple expresses their excitement to purchase the insurance.

This summarizes the main idea presented in the two body paragraphs. Details about the description of the advertisements scenario are not required in the summary because the purpose here is merely to provide examples of emotional appeals used in the company's advertisement.

Summarizing the concluding paragraph is done by taking the same steps; focusing on the main key point(s), not including details, and adding transitions whenever applicable. Here is one example of a concluding paragraph:

It follows that the focus of the advertising industry that Progressive Company employs is the emotional needs of customers as well as their background knowledge of how these needs are associated by people from different walks of life. Based on the discussion above, it can be inferred that successful advertisements are those that target people's natural interests and address as many demographic populations as possible.

This paragraph can be summarized as follows:

Targeting the feelings of the customers to promote for their insurance is Progressive Company's major trait in advertisement. The most successful strategy to use emotional appeals is to address as many groups of people as possible in order to attract the largest possible audience's attention to the product being promoted.

This summary highlights the two key points of the concluding paragraph: that Progressive Company uses emotional appeals in advertisement, and that the way these appeals target different people are used is a key factor to succeed. All in all, the whole summary of the essay can be put in one paragraph like this one:

The advertisement industry is growing and developing every day. One example is the emotional appeal strategy of advertisement that is used by Progressive Company to promote for their auto insurance. In one of their advertisements, Progressive Company targets the emotions of ladies by showing how their famous commercial girl Flo is obsessed with riding a pink pony. Similarly, the homosexual population is targeted in the Company's other advertisement in which a homosexual couple expresses their excitement to purchase the insurance. Targeting the feelings of the customers to promote for their insurance is Progressive Company's major trait in advertisement. The most successful strategy to use emotional appeals is to address as many groups of people as possible in order to attract the largest possible audience's attention to the product being promoted.

We see that summarizing an essay involves summarizing every paragraph separately, then putting the summaries together and make the necessary changes such as adding transition words and phrases. Here is another essay to summarize:

4.3.2. Summarizing an Essay (example two)

Essay

It is hard to imagine that none of us has walked by or driven by a Goodwill store at least once in their lives if not more. Goodwill is a non-profit charity organization that has thrift stores in which donated products are sold at a very affordable price. This store sells all kinds of products such as clothes, sports equipments, kitchen appliances, shoes, hardware tools, books, furniture and even automobiles. Goodwill organization provides services in the United States as well as Canada and many other countries. Goodwill business has served many people and changed their lives to the better because it provides employment opportunities for citizens with challenges, supports households with limited financial income, and helps decreasing tax liability.

It is known that some citizens encounter difficulties in getting good jobs due to reasons such as disabilities and disadvantages. Goodwill serves to provide training for those individuals to help them get good jobs and become independent. These services can elevate the citizen's self-esteem and give them the feeling that they have the ability to support themselves and become active members in the society.

Additionally, Goodwill stores are a good choice to shop for families with limited income because the prices are affordable and the items are in good condition. This place can be suitable for families with school-age children who need to get new clothes more frequently than adults. Also, Goodwill stores are the perfect option to shop for clothes that are only used at occasional times such as Halloween and camping trips.

Lastly, Goodwill organization can be beneficial in managing tax deduction. Donations citizens make to Goodwill can assist them in itemizing their tax deduction and consequently help them save money by supporting their claim to IRS. This process can make significant changes in the budgets of many households and positively affects their lives.

In sum, donating to and purchasing from Goodwill benefits all citizens involved in the process. While the money paid when making a purchase in Goodwill is used to fund training and employments to less-fortunate citizens, it is a good chance for families to buy more affordable clothes and other items. Also, donations help in tax deduction. The more citizens contribute to this charity organization, the more benefit to reach out to as many individuals as possible. It is a win-win process to them all.

Summary

After carefully reading the essay, we rephrase the main idea and key points which are stated in the thesis:

Goodwill business has served many people and changed their lives to the better because it provides employment opportunities for citizens with challenges, supports households with limited financial income, and helps decreasing tax liability.

Here is a suggested paraphrase of the thesis:

Goodwill provides benefits such as job opportunities to challenged individuals, more affordable alternatives to families with limited financial means and assessment in managing tax deduction.

Although the paraphrased thesis is not short, it is relatively shorter than the original one, and it maintains the same idea which is the most important part in summarizing.

After paraphrasing the thesis, a general introductory statement needs to be added before the thesis. This statement can be paraphrased from the beginning sentences in the introduction paragraph. These sentences provide general information about Goodwill organization. The information can be rephrased in a summarized sentence like this:

Goodwill is a non-profit charity organization that sells donated items that vary from clothes to automobiles at reasonably affordable prices.

This sentence is added to the paraphrased thesis statement to provide the following introduction to the summary:

Goodwill is a non-profit charity organization that sells donated items that vary from clothes to automobiles at reasonably affordable prices. Goodwill provides benefits such as job opportunities to challenged individuals, more affordable alternatives to families with limited financial means and assessment in managing tax deduction.

The next step is to paraphrase the key points in the first body paragraph. To accomplish this, the topic sentence in this paragraph should be located:

Goodwill serves to provide training for those individuals to help them get good jobs and become independent.

Before paraphrasing this sentence, the phrase *'those individuals'* needs more identification. This phrase refers to citizens with challenges; therefore, the rephrased sentence will look something like this:

Through Goodwill services, challenged citizens can have jobs and become independent individuals.

Similarly, this is the topic sentence of the next body paragraph:

Goodwill stores are a good choice to shop for families with limited income because the prices are affordable and the items are in good condition.

By maintain the main idea of the sentence; it can be paraphrased into the following sentence:

Families with limited income can buy inexpensive good-quality products from Goodwill.

This brings us to the final body paragraph; the following is the original topic sentence:

Donations citizens make to Goodwill can assist them in itemizing their tax deduction and consequently help them save money by supporting their claim to IRS.

Here is one suggestion on how to paraphrase this sentence:

Citizens can use their donations to Goodwill in managing their tax deduction and support their claim to IRS.

Finally, the concluding paragraph is summarized as follows:

The advantages obtained from Goodwill services can reach out to many citizens including those who make the donations.

We have all the paragraphs summarized in individual sentences. It may not be necessary to repeat the exact wording of the sentences in the summary. In this case, the information provided in these sentences is added to the paraphrased thesis statement. As a result, the summary of the whole essay can be something like the following:

Goodwill is a non-profit charity organization that sells donated items which vary from clothes to automobiles at reasonably affordable prices. Goodwill offers benefits such as job opportunities to challenged individuals who need to become independent individuals. Also, it provides inexpensive good-quality products to families with limited financial means. Finally, it assists managing tax deduction and supporting claims to IRS. The advantages obtained from Goodwill services can reach out to many citizens including those who make the donations.

The final summary paragraph shows that when summarized sentences are put together, changes to sentence structure are likely to occur. Nevertheless, the meaning must always be maintained in order for the message to be delivered accurately.

4.3.3. Summarizing an Essay (example three)

In this example, the summary is given immediately after the whole essay is presented.

Essay

Bullying seems to have existed for ever. Almost every individual has memories related to bullying either as victims or as perpetrators. Bullying is a hateful activity that is mostly practiced in schools from nursery to high school despite constant efforts to stop it. The most common kind of bullying is the physical bullying in which bigger kids try to hurt smaller more vulnerable kids. Their acts may include knocking books out of small kids' hands, pushing small kids down the stairs or slapping the door at their faces. Another kind of bullying is verbal bullying; when kids call each other names that are offensive and harsh. And finally there is the social bullying which aims at making unsecure kids feel they are unwanted in their social groups by keeping them isolated and looked down into. More recently, verbal and social bullying are used in combination to form a new kind of bullying; namely, cyber bullying. Cyber bullying includes using digital technology by tormentors who are most of the time anonymous to hurt other people, and leads them to have severe negative feeling and perform harmful actions towards themselves and others.

Cyber bullying is done by using means of electronic communication such as text messaging, emails, and social media among others to send hate messages that include texts and/or meme pictures of the victims in order to ridicule them. In most cases, some texts and meme captions become catch phrases that are labeled to the victim for a long time, and may never be forgotten. With the availability and affordability of digital technology, it has become very easy to cyber bully somebody and make it spread all over the social group in a very short time. Pictures taken secretly of the victims while using school restrooms can be used in funny memes that are sent from one device to another. It may take only few minutes for the whole school to receive these pictures and make fun of them, and the names of the perpetrators may never be known. Moreover, false information can be posted on internet platforms to purposefully humiliate the victims and spread rumors that can find their way to a large number of people who then start treating the victims accordingly. Such misbehaviors are not mere immature acts from children and teenagers. Rather, these deeds can escalate the danger of the reactions from the part of the victims and lead to serious consequences.

Repercussions resulted from cyber bullying can be severely dramatic and may likely be profound for a lifetime. Victims of cyber bullying are generally children and teenagers; very vulnerable age groups that need extra amounts of care and love instead of being exposed to any kind of violence. As a result, cyber bullying makes those kids feel depressed and may suffer from lack of enthusiasm and nervous breakdown. Worse than that, there are cases in which victims of cyber bullying end up committing suicide because they fail to live with the humiliation. Furthermore, cyber bullying victims may hurt other people, more specifically the perpetrators if their identities are revealed. There is a chance that more than one victim happens to know each other. In this case, they may form a gang on their own and decide to take revenge of the perpetrators and others who laughed at the jokes. This can end in tragic results that have damaging effects on many people.

Although there is no permanent solution to the problem of cyber bullying yet, institutions are doing their best in educating school children about the danger of cyber bullying and the importance to use technology more appropriately and wisely. It is suggested that more censorship on social media is practiced in order to monitor kids' actions online. Also, adult supervision is highly encouraged on their kids who use social media. However, one of the best possible solutions to cyber bullying and to other kinds of bullying is in encouraging students to spend less time in using the technology and more time in other productive activities such as sports, small chores, or even jobs if they are old enough. Providing emotional support to teenagers is important to promote their positive feelings of the world and make them assure that they are individuals who can be loved and cared for and that they do matter to others.

Summary

Bullying is still on the increase, only it takes different forms in recent days. After being mostly physical, it has become more verbal and social in the form of cyber bullying. Cyber bullying is done by sending text messages and pictures via digital technology. Such a practice is very affordable and spreadable and can have negative effects on the victims. These effects are so severely painful that they may lead to tragic consequences such as suicide attempts or hurting the perpetrators and possibly other people. Affective procedures should be taken to prevent cyber bullying, for example applying more adult censorship when kids use social media and internet platforms. Also, engaging the kids in other activities like sports can be a good solution to make them feel more secure and self-fulfilled.

Exercise 1. Summarize the following paragraphs:

1. Qais is a successful physiotherapist who has achieved a lot as a student. He was born in Misrata in 1986. He attended Misrata Science High school from 2011 to 2005.Upon graduation from High school, he got college admission in the Faculty of Medical Technology in Misrata University and graduated with a Bachelor degree of Science in Physiotherapy. At that moment, he knew that this major would help him build up his future academic and professional careers. In 2015, he was granted a full scholarship to pursue his Master's degree in Sultan Zain Abidin University in Malaysia. As always, Qais was a hard-working student with a lot of ambition and future plans. During his Master's program, he published a serious of articles in different journals such as Scopus and ISI. Moreover, he participated in science conferences in Malaysia and Indonesia. Because his conference participations were uniquely distinguished, he won the award of Excellence and Innovation at the conference in Penang in 2017. One of Qais's great achievements is the book he published about managing and preventing low back pain. He is currently working on his second book which he desires to publish in the near future. It is Qais's belief that he always has something to offer in his field of study that can contribute to the development of the science of Physiotherapy.

Qais, a physiotherapist

2. One of the functions of the human brain is to constitute a boundary between the five senses to make them separate and refined. However, there is a case in which no boundary is established between

the senses; and therefore, more than one sense are blended together to perceive the surrounding environment. This condition is referred to as synesthesia. For example, a synesthetic individual may say that the sound of the door bill is red or that number 7 has a nice smell. Interestingly, we all have experienced synesthesia when we were little infants, and as we get older, the boundaries between the senses become more refined. The most common type of synesthesia is the blending between auditory stimulation and visual sensation. For instance, a person who has synesthesia may see music instead of hearing it. They may say something like: this orchestra has an orange pattern! Another thing to know about synesthesia is that it is systematic; i.e. the perception does not change. An individual with synesthesia who believes number 7 has a nice smell will always think that at all times and ages. It is not easy to specify the number of people who have this condition possibly because some of those who have it do not recognize they do.

3. What is beauty? The general consensus throughout the world when the word *beauty* comes up is that it is all about appearance. There are cultural differences on how to perceive this appearance based on culture-specific standards of beauty. The general mainstream perception of beauty in most parts of Western World is related to being tall, slim with high cheek bones, delicate features, and small waist. As a result, women in these societies tend to undergo excessive diets and exhaust themselves exercising on a daily basis. Their utmost dream is to obtain the perfect ideal figure they need for a job like super models or simply to draw attention and enhance their self-esteem as they get admiring comments on their perfect shapes by men and women alike. On the other hand, beauty standards in some tribes in Africa, for example, are based on heaviness; the heavier the body the more beautiful. Teenage girls and young ladies in Nigeria go to what is called *fattening room* in order to gain as many pounds as possible to obtain the perfect curvy figure. All the lady has to do in this room is eat and sleep until she reaches the perfect weight and be ready to marry. Color of the skin is one important measure of beauty in China. You will never see a Chinese lady using spray tan or get sun-tanning unless she has spent some time of her life in a Western culture. In relation to this discussion, it is not fair to make judgments on the appearance of ladies based on culture-specific traits of beauty. In other words, every lady is beautiful because every lady fits the standards of beauty in some culture.

4. Have you ever witnessed an incident in which somebody is in trouble and you hesitate to intervene because you want to wait for someone else to step in? This phenomenon is known as *bystander effect*; a term used to describe the state of not intervening to help one individual or more in distress, waiting for someone else to imitate. It is said that the greater the crowd the less likely for observers to intervene in the emergency situation. Therefore, the amount of time taken to step in, if ever, depends on the number of people witnessing the incident. Bystander effect is not recent; back in 1964, a 28 year-old lady named Kitty Genovese was stabbed to death in front of the building where she lived in New York City. Despite her constant calls for help as she was lying down on the floor, no one in the building who heard her cries moved to help her or even called for help until about half an hour after the attack had started. Studies reveal two major reasons for the occurrence of bystander effect. The first reason is that the presence of a crowd in the scene establishes a diffusion of responsibility. Due to the presence of other witnesses, no one takes personal responsibility to get involved in the issue. The second reason is related to social influence that requires the person to monitor the behaviors of surrounding people and act accordingly. Resistance to help somebody who needs assistance, though, still exists, can be reduced from the part of the victim by purposefully signaling out one person from the crowd and ask for their help immediately.

5. Individuals who experience shocking unforgettable events may constantly reexperience the pain of these events. Reliving traumatic experience is one symptom of a disorder referred to as Post-Traumatic Stress Disorder (PTSD); a condition in which memories of pain caused by bad situations are overgeneralized and prevent the individual from coping with their stress and maintain a good mental well-being. Individuals who suffer from PTSD experience different ways of reliving traumatic incidents. For example, painful memories can be relived through a flashback. The individual may have a strong feeling that they are back in the incident once again, and they even feel the same pain and stress they had the first time. This can possibly make them resistant to deal with anything or anybody that reminds them of the incident. Another way to relive the past bad memories is through nightmares, which leave the person sleep-deprived or even cause insomnia. Incidents that cause the symptoms of PTSD are found among victims of severely harmful actions such as rape, child abuse, witnessing a murder (especially as a child), or attending war. Having a recollection of annoying events may be hard to overcome either immediately after the shock or later in life.

--------◆◆◆◆◆◆--------

Exercise 2. Summarize the following essays:

1. There are still misunderstandings surrounding disability which is perceived as equal to incapability and being permanently sick. The word *disability* itself represents a misunderstanding of its own. It is believed that individuals with physical challenges are incapable to live up to the standards of an average able person. Individuals with certain disabilities have the same natural needs and health hardship as individuals who do not have such disabilities. In other words, disability is a natural characteristic of being human and it is definitely one part of human experience. It is harsh and offensive to look at them as handicapped because the fact is they are not. Stereotypical judgments are made about citizens with physical challenges depicting them as being incapable and vulnerable. Despite the recent emphasis on the rights of physically-challenged citizens, myths and misconceptions that surround citizens with physical challenges still exist. Even if they have jobs, those individuals are frequently surrounded with unfair misconceptions. There are misunderstanding about physically-challenged employees in work places which include higher absentee rates, success at work, and expensive accommodations.

It is said that absentee rate is higher among physically-challenged employees than their other non-disabled colleagues. This myth conflicts findings of research conducted by DuPont firm which states that the absentee rate of non-disabled employees is not different from disabled ones if not higher. This is confirmed by many employers who not only experience less absenteeism from the part of the disabled employees, but also higher productivity. It follows that being an individual with physical challenges does not mean that this person is frequently sick and required sick leaves. Likewise, being a person with no disability does not indicate adherence to full attendance at work.

Another misunderstanding about the physically-challenged employees is that they have to always be successful at work. This opposes human nature in which failure is present as much as success is. The chance for disabled employees not to be very successful in their work is no different from the chance of their non-disabled colleagues. Failure and success at work are part of making a career and they are always present in the employees' lives; therefore, employees with disabilities seek a high degree of quality of life and this does not happen without facing challenges. In this respect, all employees should have equal rights to get promotions, raises, and other job benefits regardless of any physical challenges that might seem to make the job performed uneasily.

A third false myth perceived about disabled employees is that they require certain accommodations that are costly. It is reported that more than 70% of employers state that their disabled employees did not need special accommodations, and that in case certain accommodations are required they are not expensive. Special services and devices disabled employees need can be offered at affordable prices. For example, adding ramps near the stairs is not very expensive and it is suitable to be used by employees in wheelchairs in addition to employees who need to use carts at work. Moreover, work places are already equipped with facilities that are convenient for all the employees such as elevators and electronic doors as well as the facilities provided in restrooms.

Generally speaking, the fact that employees with disabilities have a high attendance rate, face challenges to be successful at work and do not need expensive accommodations require the term *disabled* to be changed into *differently-abled*. Having a disability is no different from being left-handed and hence employees with disabilities should be considered as being differently capable of doing their jobs rather than suspecting their ability to perform. In fact, employees with disability can be a source of creativity and productivity and can motivate other non-disabled employees to perform their jobs more efficiently.

2. In 2014, many people all over the world were waiting for the release of IPhone 6. Customers were so excited for the thin shapes and big screens of the device that despite the costly price, they waited in long lines in front of Apple stores from early hours in the morning to purchase the device. However, it did not take long for some customers to announce controversial complaints about IPhone 6 Plus devices. The problem, they referred to as a crisis, was that the IPhone 6 Plus devices those customers had purchased bended after they were put in back pockets. Apple had no alternative but to act immediately to resolve the issue and fix the problem of IPhone 6 Plus bending.

The complaints were first reported via social media on Facebook and Twitter. These complains came out following the reports provided by Apple that IPhone 6 devices were extremely robust and solid after tests, that did not include the bending feature, were performed on IPhone 6 phones. There were hundreds of posts and tweets from owners of IPhone 6 Plus phones stating that these devices started to bend after one week of use. Although the number of complaining customers is very little as compared with other satisfied ones, the issue was not to ignore because it was not the first time for Apple to experience such a problem. Similar reports were made in 2010 regarding IPhone 4 as well as in 2013 about IPhone 5. Furthermore, these complains were also recorded to be made about devices produced by other companies such as Blackberry Q10 and Galaxy S4. It is necessary to know the reason behind such deformation of one of Apple's products.

The IPhone 6 Plus was manufactured from solid aluminum that was not very strong in the volume button area where the bending takes place. However, this does not imply that the device would always bend from that area after being used. IPhone 6 Plus was designed in a way that could endure daily regular use. The tests conducted on the device before being released into the market included testing the strength ability of the device, and resistance of pressure caused by bending while setting. All results confirm that the deformation of the IPhone 6 Plus was not associated with its design; rather, it was related to the way it was handled.

Suggestions were provided by Apple Company about the proper ways to handle IPhone 6 Plus in order to avoid the occurrence of device deformation. The major idea was to choose a better way to carry the phone around other than using the back pocket. For example, top garment pockets could be a better way to carry the phone on their person as it is less tight and easier to reach out than the back pocket. Another suggestion was to carry the phone in the back pocket but to avoid sitting and leaning forward with the phone in the back pockets of the pants; placing it on a table or holding it in hand while sitting was a good idea. Besides these suggestions, Apple announced to customers with deformed IPhone 6 Plus phones to bring the devices to an Apple store with the receipts in order to get satisfactory compensations.

The huge news about the release of IPhone 6 and IPhone 6 Plus was not quite ceased until the huge news about the bending deformation took place. Apparently, more tests and feedback were required from Apple before releasing the phone. The fact that most people carry their phones in their back pockets was supposed to be considered more thoroughly. In other words, the problem with IPhone 6 Plus bending was in how it was used not in how it was made. No matter how solid the IPhone 6 Plus or other phone device was and no matter how much it could tolerate heavy weights, the way the device is used and handled could cause damages to it if not used properly.

3. We all like listening to music for fun and relaxation because it helps raising happiness and spirits and soothing the soul. Although not everybody can carry a tune or play a musical instrument, almost everybody is connected to some kind of music to which they associate good memories with people, places, etc. Music is connected to positive mood. People listen to music all the time everywhere; to get through the daily commute, to help stay energetic during workout, and to make daily chores more enjoyable among other things. Since music is a source of comfort and relieve, it is believed to be a good therapeutic strategy that helps in the healing process of some diseases and also decreasing disease symptoms.

    Despite the positive influence of complementary therapeutic kinds of treatment such as yoga, meditation and art, music is said to have the most affective results due to the fact that it is more transmissible, free of charge or more affordable, accessible by everybody, and does not require exhausting physical and/or mental efforts. Such reasons are investigated in studies which emphasize the usability of music in healing many medical conditions.

    One example of the benefit of music in healing is using it to treat lost speech. Lost speech results from having a stroke or traumatic damage to the left-brain area which is responsible for speech. Music stimulates different parts of the brains and motivates the desire to sing along and use our voices. Patients who suffer from lost speech can first start by singing their thoughts as a way to communicate until they gradually restore their ability to move their lips and tongue to speak. This strategy has proven the advantageous effects of combining neuroscience medical treatment and music therapy regardless of the differences these two disciplines have.

    Another way to use music as therapy is to reduce anxiety caused by cancer treatment. Research has shown that music cannot contribute in the medical treatment of cancer or prevent it from happening. However, it is proven that music helps cancer patients have better quality of life and reduce the stress, anxiety, and nausea caused by side effects of cancer treatment such as chemotherapy and radiotherapy. According to studies, it is reported that listening to music can increase the production of dopamine; an endorphin that is associated to feelings of pleasure.

Music functions as a healing therapy to diseases by lifting up the spirits of the patients and making them in a positive mood required for responding to medical treatment. With the different types of music, there is always at least one type in favor for patients to listen and find some kind of connection to. In addition to enjoying the music, it plays an important role in reducing stress and giving us energy required to heal from diseases and side effects caused by treatment of diseases.

4. The following is an article titled *Oral and Maxillofacial Surgery Unit at Misrata Central Hospital* by Dr. Yaser and Dr. Maan, two professional dentists in Misrata Medical Center who are also researchers in the field of Oral and Maxillofacial Surgery. Read the article carefully and summaries the main points into a shorts text.

Note: There is no need to summarize the information in table 4.

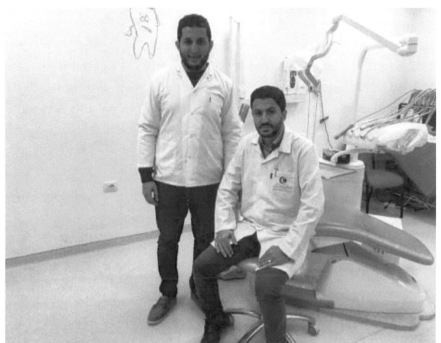

Dr. Maan and Dr.Yaser.

Article

Oral and Maxillofacial Surgery Unit at Misrata Central Hospital

Misrata Central Hospital, located in the center of the city of Misrata, was launched in 1975 in an area of approximately 12 thousand square meters. It is classified as one of the service facilities of the city which contains 720 beds in addition to several medical departments as well as assistance and management medical offices. Moreover, the number of staff working in all specialties in the hospital is 1679 employees. The hospital also has 13 administrative offices, 8 departments each of which contains units to conduct medical work. A decision is recently issued by the Prime Minister to officially approve the hospital as Misrata Medical Center and raise its clinical capacity to 1000 beds upon the completion of maintenance of the building. Misrata Medical Center has developed significant services in the field of oral and maxillofacial surgery which is recognized as a prime need to the citizens along with other medical necessities.

The oral and maxillofacial surgery unit was first introduced at Misrata Central Hospital on March 1st, 2016 with one oral and maxillofacial surgeon and four doctors major in oral and jaw surgery. On April 1st, 2016, the outpatient clinic for oral and maxillofacial surgery was inaugurated to receive daily cases of oral and maxillofacial injuries resulted from the various accidents such as road traffic accidents, work injuries, sports injuries, various falls, infections, etc. urgent surgical operations are carried out regularly around the clock in the operations unit of the trauma and emergency department of the hospital. The unit covers all injuries resulting from explosions and bullets of all kinds and follows up on all cases until full recovery is obtained. Also, it saved a lot of cases suffered from the active bleeding or that suffocated from spreading of infections. Furthermore, the oral and maxillofacial surgery unit has recently introduced the reception and treatment of oral congenital anomalies in children such as the harelip and the cleft palate.

After the visit of a high-level delegation from the Arab Council for Medical Specializations, the face and maxillofacial surgery unit in Misrata Medical Center has been accredited as a training center of the Arab Fellowship for Facial and Maxillofacial Surgery. One result of this is recognizing Dr. Yasser Howayw as the Head of the Unit of the first Arab Fellowship Training Supervisor in the Central Region. Followed after that, six doctors were admitted to the academic and practical training program of the Arab Fellowship for Oral and Maxillofacial Surgery of 2018.

The unit hosts a number of consultants periodically from inside and outside the country. The number of specialists in the unit has been increased to two oral and maxillofacial Surgery as specialists, and the number of doctors of oral and Maxillofacial Surgery as a junior has reached up to seven doctors. On January 2017, a dental clinic was added to the unit, with 3 professional dentists to receive and treat regular dental cases.

It is the desire of the ambitious doctors working in the Unit of Oral and Maxillofacial surgery that the unit becomes the core of Misrata Central Hospital to cover all the cases in the region nearby. Table 4 represents explanatory information of the type and number of operations carried out in the unit from January 2016 to November 2017.

TYPE OF OP.	QUNTITY OF OP.
RTA	89
FULL DOWN	35
GUN SHOOT	33
BLAST INJURY	27
SEPSIS	25
PATHOLOGY	23
SPORTS INJURY	18
CONGINTAL ANAMOLIES	15
ASSULT	10
BLEEDING DISORDERS	3
TOTAL OF MAJOR SURGERY	278
TOTAL OF MINOR SURGERY	320
TOTAL OF DENTAL CASES	840

Table 4, type and number of operations carried out in the face and maxillofacial surgery unit in Misrata Medical Center from January 2016 to November 2017

Chapter Five

Compare and Contrast Essays

"We're both Thieves, Harvey Swick. I take time. You take lives. But in the end we're the same: both Thieves of Always"

Clive Barker

Writing compare and contrast essays is one kind of creative writing which consists of two components associated to aspects about the topic. The first is comparing the similarities these aspects have in common; the second is contrasting the differences between these aspects. Some similarities and differences already exist as general characteristics of the items being drawn parallel. Others, on the other hand, are related to the writer's understanding of the topic.

For example, if we desire to make a comparison between online shopping and store shopping, one of the overt distinctions is that online shopping can be done at home whereas store shopping cannot. However, the amount of money spent in each kind of shopping is relevant; in that, it depends on the customer not on the product. We cannot give an absolute judgment about either kind of shopping regarding money spending because consumption is performed by the customer and every customer is different in their way of spending. As a result, a person who tends to spend a lot of money in shopping will see money spending as a common feature between online shopping and store shopping. This may not be the same for another customer who is not a big spender in shopping.

5.1. Transitions in Compare and Contrast Essays

Transition words used in compare and contrast essays link sentences in order to emphasize similarities and/or differences between ideas. Table 5 contains a list of these transitions.

	Transitions	Examples
Comparison	Similarly, likewise, compared to, at the same time, the same manner/ way, in a similar fashion/manner/ way, by the same token, as well as, just/same as, correspondingly.	- I love action movies; likewise, my friends enjoy these movies a lot. - The capital city encourages volunteer work for better chances of future jobs. In a similar way, the second largest city has started promoting for volunteer activities.
Contrast	However, but, on the other hand, in contrast, unlike, even though, rather, in a different manner/ way, nevertheless, whereas, on the contrary, contrary to.	- The new plan highlights the core reason of the project, whereas the old one puts all the focus on supporting details. - Contrary to last semester, the classes I enroll for this semester are not very demanding and time consuming.

Table 5 comparison and contrast transition words

Here are example sentences which are combined with these transition words

1. It is cold this week. Next week will be cold too.
- It is cold this week; *similarly*, next week will be cold too.

2. One businessman wants to purchase the property in order to build a big shopping mall. Another businessman wants to buy the same property to make a new housing complex.
- One businessman wants to purchase the property in order to build a big shopping mall. *In contrast*, another businessman wants to buy the same property to make a new housing complex.

3. When she was a teenager, Sally was a wonderful dancer and she won a full scholarship to finish her education in college. Her granddaughter shows real talent in dancing and is constantly improving.
- When she was a teenager, Sally was a wonderful dancer and she won a full scholarship to finish her education in college. *Likewise*, her granddaughter shows real talent in dancing and is constantly improving.

4. He got C in the test because he did not study hard. He also failed to turn his paper on time and ended up failing the class.
- He got C in the test because he did not study hard. *In a similar manner*, he also failed to turn his paper on time and ended up failing the class.

5. She went to culinary class and became a good chef. Her friend did not like culinary class so she decided to drop it and take a computer class instead.
- She went to culinary class and became a good chef. *On the contrary*, her friend did not like culinary class so she decided to drop it and take a computer class instead.

6. I am not good at making dessert. My skills in baking pastry are unreliable.

- I am not good at making dessert; *by the same token*, my skills in baking pastry are unreliable.

These transition words are important in improving the quality of the essay and make it more enjoyable to read. The following paragraphs demonstrate the use of these transition words.

5.2. How to Write a Compare and Contrast Essay

1. The first thing in writing a compare and contrast essay is to organize the ideas in the brainstorming step into three categories as shown in Venn diagram 1

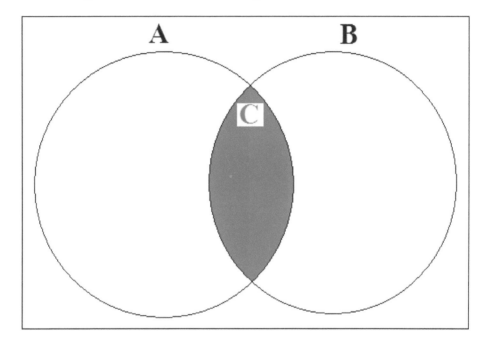

Diagram 1 Compare and contrast diagram

As diagram 1 shows, when brainstorming for a compare and contrast essay, the first thing to do is to classify the points intended to be discussed in three categories: category A is only for the characteristics that belong to A, Category B is for characteristics that belong to B, and category C is specified for characteristics that A and B have in common.

Another way to classify these three categories is by organizing them in a table such as table 6.

Category A	Both	Category B

Table 6, compare and contrast table

5.2.1. Compare and Contrast Essay Outline

There are two ways to organize the outline: block outline, and point-by-point outline. In block outline, all the similarities between the two categories are listed first followed by the difference, or vice versa. In point-by-point outline, each point of similarity between the two categories is followed by a point of difference. The later is used when the comparison is made by presenting characteristics and their opposites. Here are examples of the two kinds of outline:

5.2.1.1. Block Outline

I.   Introduction

    a. General review
    b. Thesis

II.   Body

    a. Topic sentence (differences)
        i.   Supporting detail # 1
        ii.   Supporting detail # 2
        iii. Supporting detail # 3
    b. Topic sentence (Similarities)
        i.   Supporting detail # 1
        ii.   Supporting detail # 2
        iii. Supporting detail # 3

III. Conclusion

    a. Thesis restatement
    b. General review

5.2.1.2. Point-by-point Outline

I.   Introduction

    a. General Review
    b. Thesis

II. Body

    a. Topic sentence (differences # 1)

        i.   Supporting detail # 1

        ii.   Supporting detail # 2

        iii.   Supporting detail # 3

    b. Topic sentence (difference # 2)

        i.   Supporting detail # 1

        ii.   Supporting detail # 2

        iii.   Supporting detail # 3

    c. Topic sentence (difference # 3)

        i.   Supporting detail # 1

        ii.   Supporting detail # 2

        iii.   Supporting detail # 3

    d. Topic sentence (similarity # 1)

        i.   Supporting detail # 1

        ii.   Supporting detail # 2

        iii.   Supporting detail # 3

    e. Topic sentence (similarity # 2)

        i.   Supporting detail # 1

        ii.   Supporting detail # 2

        iii.   Supporting detail # 3

    f. Topic sentence (similarity # 3)

        i.   Supporting detail # 1

        ii.   Supporting detail # 2

        iii.   Supporting detail # 3

III. Conclusion

    a. Thesis restatement

    b. General review

5. 3. Compare and Contrast Essay (example one)

For example, if the topic is to compare and contrast between online shopping vs. Store shopping, diagram 2 can be filled as follows:

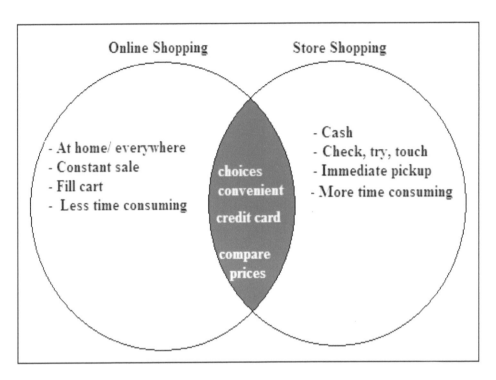

Diagram 2, Compare and contrast: online shopping vs. Store shopping

The same information is organized in table 7.

Online Shopping	Both	Store Shopping
- At home/ everywhere - Sale - Fill cart - Less time consuming	- Choices - Convenient - Credit Card - Compare prices	- Cash - Check, try, touch - Immediate pick up - More time consuming

Table 7, Compare and contrast: online shopping vs. Store shopping

2. The next step is to build the thesis Statement. The main idea is about the differences and similarities between online shopping and store shopping. As a result, the thesis statement can be formed like this:
As there are many features in common between online shopping and store shopping, there are differences between them as well.

3. The third step is to formulate an outline of the essay. Here are examples of the two kinds of outline:

Block Outline

Outline:

I.   Introduction

    a. General review

    b. Thesis (As there are many features in common between online shopping and store shopping, there are differences between them as well).

II.   Body

    a. Topic sentence (differences between online shopping and store shopping).

    i. Supporting detail #1 (location)

        1.   Online shopping (everywhere)

        2.   Store shopping (at the store).

    ii. Supporting detail # 2 (time).

        1.   Online shopping (all the time).

        2.   Store shopping (store hours).

    iii. Supporting detail # 3 (check the product).

        1.   Online shopping (inapplicable).

        2.   Store shopping (possible).

    iv. Supporting detail #4 (prices).

        1.   Online shopping (frequent sales).

        2.   Store shopping (less frequent sales).

    v. Supporting detail # 5 (cart).

        1.   Online shopping (unlimited fill).

        2.   Store shopping (limited fill).

    vi. Supporting detail # 6 (payment).

        1.   Online shopping (credit card).

        2.   Store shopping (credit card/ cash).

    vii. Supporting detail # 7 (delivery).

        1.   Online shopping (at the door).

        2.   Store shopping (personal pick up).

    b. Topic sentence (Similarities between online shopping and store shopping).

    i. Supporting detail # 1

        1.   Choices

    ii. Supporting detail # 2

        2.   Convenience.

    iii. Supporting detail # 3

       3.   Credit card

III.   Conclusion

  a. Thesis restatement

  b. General review

Point-by-Point Outline

I.   Introduction

  a. General Review

  b. Thesis (As there are many features in common between online shopping and store shopping, there are differences between them as well).

II.   Body

  a. Topic sentence (differences # 1) (Location).

    i.   Online shopping (everywhere).

    ii.   Store shopping (store hours).

  b. Topic sentence (difference # 2) (Price).

    i.   Online shopping (frequent sales).

    ii.   Store shopping (less frequent sales).

  c. Topic sentence (difference # 3) (Cart).

    i.   Online shopping (unlimited fill).

    ii.   Store shopping (limited fill).

  d. Topic sentence (difference # 4) (Payment).

    i.   Online shopping (credit card).

    ii.   Store shopping (credit card/ cash).

  e. Topic sentence difference # 5) (delivery).

    i.   Online shopping (at the door).

    ii.   Store shopping (personal pick up).

  f. Topic sentence (similarity # 1)

    i.   Supporting detail # 1 (Choices).

  g. Topic sentence (similarity # 2)

    i.   Supporting detail # 1 (Convenience)

III. Conclusion

  a. Thesis restatement

  b. General review

Now that the outlines are ready, the next step is to write the essay. There are two types of organization to follow in essay structure; block organization and point-by-point organization. We will start with block organization.

Block Essay

Following the block outline provided above, the first paragraph to work on is the introduction. Based on outline structure, the introduction goes from general to specific and narrows down until we reach to the thesis. Here is an example of the introductory paragraph:

Shopping is always seen as one of the fun activities people like to do. New products of everything have their big fans who keep themselves updated with the latest fashion. After online shopping services are made, more options have been added to shopping to make it more convenient and available to all customers every time and everywhere. Nowadays, customers have the chance to do shopping both on line and in stores with many benefits obtained from both ways of shopping. As there are many features in common between online shopping and store shopping, there are differences between them as well.

The step that comes next is to work on body paragraphs, which are two according to the block outline. The first body paragraph discusses the differences between online shopping and store shopping. The information in the outline is used to form a paragraph such as the following:

One of the differences between online shopping and store shopping is that online shopping can be done at home or any other place at any time suitable for the customer. In contrary, store shopping is done by the customer being physically present at the store during limited store hours. This makes shopping in stores more time consuming than shopping online; in fact, shopping in stores requires allocating specific time for it whereas shopping online can be done while doing another activity such as taking the bus or having lunch. Nevertheless, it is believed that shopping in stores is worth the time because it gives the customer the chance to physically check the products by touching and feeling them and even trying them on if possible; an advantage that is not available in online stores. Another difference is related to the prices; although there are affordable stores both online and on the ground, sales chances are found more frequently in online stores. This could be related to the fact that browsing online for the best price is faster than physically going from one store to another. As a result, finding the cheapest price in online stores is possible at a reasonable period of time. When it comes to filling the cart, there is no limit to the number of products that can be added to online carts; however, this option is a little hard when shopping in stores. The payment for the products for both kinds of shopping is processed by the use of credit cards; with paying in cash is an option available only in store shopping. While delivering the products is performed immediately by personal pick up in store shopping, it takes some time for products ordered online to be delivered at the customer's door.

Similar work is done in the second body paragraph which focuses on the similarities between online and store shopping:

Along with differences, online and store shopping have a number of similarities. One feature the two kinds of shopping share is the availability of a variety of choices. Interestingly, stores on the ground have websites in which they show all their products and new arrivals; as a result, checking the new products of online and ground stores is available at the convenience of the customers. This enables customers to compare prices between stores on ground and stores on websites and choose the price that suits them the most. Online shopping as well as store shopping provide a source of convenience and relieve to customers. For some customers, going to stores in person and checking the products is their way to relax and vent some stress. Likewise; the same reason can interest other customers who desire to relieve anxiety by browsing through online stores. One final example about the similarities between shopping online and shopping in stores is the use of credit cards as a payment option. This procedure makes shopping easier, faster, and available to a large number of customers.

The next paragraph to write is the concluding paragraph in which the topic is wrapped up. As explained in chapter 1, the conclusion restates the main idea and moves to the broader perspective of the topic. The following paragraph can function as a conclusion to our topic:

Generally speaking, despite the differences between online shopping and store shopping, both of them serve the needs of their customers and provide options that suit different personalities. It follows that both kinds of shopping function in combination to provide satisfactory options which always work for customers who want to enjoy shopping and keep acquainted with new comings in the market.

Now that all the paragraphs are built, they can be put together as one essay:

Shopping is always seen as one of the fun activities people like to do. New products of everything have their big fans who keep themselves updated with the latest fashion. After online shopping services are made, more options have been added to shopping to make it more convenient and available to all customers every time and everywhere. Nowadays, customers have the chance to do shopping both on line and at stores with many benefits obtained from both ways of shopping. As there are many features in common between online shopping and store shopping, there are differences between them as well.

One of the differences between online shopping and store shopping is that online shopping can be done at home or any other place at any time suitable for the customer, unlike store shopping which is done by the customer being physically present at the store during limited store hours. This makes shopping in stores more time consuming than shopping online; in fact, shopping in stores requires allocating specific time for it whereas shopping online can be done while doing another activity such as taking the bus or having lunch. Nevertheless, it is believed that shopping in stores is worth the time because it gives the customer the chance to physically check the products by touching and feeling them and even trying them on if possible; an advantage that is not available in online store. Another difference is related to the prices; although there are affordable stores both online and on the ground, sales chances are found more frequently in online stores. This could be related to the fact that browsing online for the best price is faster than physically going from one store to another. As a result, finding the cheapest price in online stores is possible at a reasonable period of time. When it comes to filling the cart, there is no limit to the number of products that can be added to online carts; however, this option is a little hard when shopping in stores. The payment for the products for both kinds of shopping is processed by the use of credit cards; with paying in cash is an option available only in store shopping. While delivering the products is performed immediately by personal pick up in store shopping, it takes a considerable long time for products ordered online to be delivered at the customer's door.

Along with differences, online and store shopping have a number of similarities. One feature the two kinds of shopping share is the availability of a variety of choices. Interestingly, stores on the ground have websites in which they show all their products and new arrivals; as a result, checking the new products of online and ground stores is available at the convenience of the customers. This enables customers to compare prices between stores on ground and stores on websites and choose the price that suits them the most. Online shopping as well as store shopping provide a source of convenience and relieve to customers. For some customers, going to stores in person and checking the products is their way to relax and vent some stress a. Likewise; the same reason can interest other customers who desire to relieve anxiety by browsing through online stores. One final example about the similarities between shopping online and shopping in stores is the use of credit cards as a payment option. This procedure makes shopping easier, faster, and available to a large number of customers.

Generally speaking, despite the differences between online shopping and store shopping, both of them serve the needs of their customers and provide options that suit different personalities. It follows that both kinds of shopping function in combination to provide satisfactory options which always work for customers who want to enjoy shopping and keep acquainted with new comings in the market.

Point-by- point Essay

This is the other way to write a compare and contrast essay. Regarding our topic, the introduction and the conclusion paragraphs are the same as the ones in the block essay. The work here is on the body paragraphs that need to be rearranged in the point-by-point style. In this case, each point of similarities and differences is set in a separate paragraph. For example, when discussing the difference between online shopping and store shopping in terms of location, this information is provided in a separate paragraph, such as the following:

There are many differences between online shopping and store shopping. In terms of location, online shopping is done at home and other places, while store shopping is done at the store on the ground. Although stores have websites through which customers can browse and purchase items, the chance is always available for customers to go to the store and do the purchase in person.

The next paragraph discusses another point of difference; namely, prices. Here is an example paragraph:

Price is another difference online and store shopping. Although the difference may not be very significant in some cases, the frequent sale chance provided in online stores makes it more appealing for customers to consider online shopping more often. Furthermore, comparing prices in online stores is easier and less time consuming than comparing prices in stores on the ground. In addition, the decision to buy a product, even though is not usually immediate in two kinds of shopping, it can take longer when shopping online because the item can be saved in the cart for a later time in the future.

This last sentence can function as a bridge to the next paragraph which discusses filling the cart in shopping.

Regarding the cart, online shopping allows for unlimited amount of products for a long time; such an option is not usually available in stores where carts can be loaded with a limited number of products. Additionally, when filling the cart in online stores, the customer gets to check the prices every once in a while until it drops to a good payable amount. Such a service may not be available at this convenience in stores on the ground.

Difference in payment is the next point to discuss in the paragraph that follows:

Although credit cards are used for both kinds of shopping, paying in cash is only available in store shopping. The way of payment can be a key factor in choosing between shopping online and shopping in stores. For some customers, paying with a credit card is more convenient because it saves the trouble and worry for the customers to carry money on their person. However, other customers believe that carrying cash in shopping reduces the temptation to spending money. The later kind of customers is likely to shop in stores rather than online.

One last difference between online shopping and store shopping is the way the product is picked up. In online shopping, the purchased items take a period of time to be delivered at the door of the customer. This period of time varies from one week or less to a month or more. In some cases, the item is not delivered at the customer's door; rather, it is delivered to the postal service office and the customer is required to go to the office to pick up the item. In contrast, when shopping in a store, the items are purchased, paid for and picked up in person.

Now the discussion moves to the similarities between online shopping and store shopping. According to the point-by-point outline, the points of similarity are: choices and convenience. Information about each one of them is provided in a separate paragraph. The information about the similarities provided in the block essay can be used here. The following is the paragraph about choices in online and store shopping:

Along with differences, online and store shopping have a number of similarities. One feature the two kinds of shopping share is the availability of a variety of choices. Interestingly, stores on the ground have websites in which they show all their products and new arrivals; as a result, checking the new products of online and ground stores is available at the convenience of the customers. This offers multiple resources for customers to find the items they look for.

The following paragraph is the last in the body part. It explains another similarity between online and store shopping regarding convenience:

Another similarity between online shopping and store shopping is related to convenience. Online shopping as well as store shopping provide a source of convenience and relieve to customers. For some customers, going to stores in person and checking the products is their way to relax and vent some stress. Likewise; the same reason can interest other customers who desire to relieve anxiety by browsing through online stores.

By adding the same introduction and conclusion provided in the block essay, the following is the complete point-by-point essay:

Shopping is always seen as one of the fun activities people like to do. New products of everything have their big fans who keep themselves updated with the latest fashion. After online shopping services are made, more options have been added to shopping to make it more convenient and available to all customers every time and everywhere. Nowadays, customers have the chance to do shopping both on line and at stores with many benefits obtained from both ways of shopping. As there are many features in common between online shopping and store shopping, there are differences between them as well.

There are many differences between online shopping and store shopping. In terms of location, online shopping is done at home and other places, while store shopping is done at the store on the ground. Although stores have websites through which customers can browse and purchase items, the chance is always available for customers to go to the store and do the purchase in person.

Price is another difference online and store shopping. Although the difference may not be very significant in some cases, the frequent sale chance provided in online stores makes it more appealing for customers to consider online shopping more often. Furthermore, comparing prices in online stores is easier and less time consuming than comparing prices in stores on the ground. In addition, the decision to buy a product, even though is not usually immediate in two kinds of shopping, it can take longer when shopping online because the item can be saved in the cart for a later time in the future.

Regarding the cart, online shopping allows for unlimited amount of products for a long time; such an option is not usually available in stores where carts can be loaded with a limited number of products. Additionally, when filling the cart on online stores, the customer gets to check the prices every once in a while until it drops to a good payable amount. Such a service may not be available at this convenience in stores on the ground.

Although credit cards are used for both kinds of shopping, paying in cash is only available in store shopping. The way of payment can be a key factor in choosing between shopping online and shopping in stores. For some customers, paying with a credit card is more convenient because it saves the trouble and worry for the customers to carry money on their person. However, other customers believe that carrying cash in shopping reduces the temptation to spending money. The later kind of customers is likely to shop in stores rather than online.

One last difference between online shopping and store shopping is the way the product is picked up. In online shopping, the purchased items take a period of time to be delivered at the door of the customer. This period of time varies from one week or less to a month or more. In some cases, the item is not delivered at the customer's door; rather, it is delivered to the postal service office and the customer is required to go to the office to pick up the item. In contrast, when shopping in a store, the items are purchased, paid for and picked up in person.

Along with differences, online and store shopping have a number of similarities. One feature the two kinds of shopping share is the availability of a variety of choices. Interestingly, stores on the ground have websites in which they show all their products and new arrivals; as a result, checking the new products of online and ground stores is available at the convenience of the customers. This offers multiple resources for customers to find the items they look for.

Another similarity between online shopping and store shopping is related to convenience. Online shopping as well as store shopping provide a source of convenience and relieve to customers. For some customers, going to stores in person and checking the products is their way to relax and vent some stress. Likewise; the same reason can interest other customers who desire to relieve anxiety by browsing through online stores.

Generally speaking, despite the differences between online shopping and store shopping, both of them serve the needs of their customers and provide options that suit different personalities. It follows that both kinds of shopping function in combination to provide satisfactory options which always work for customers who want to enjoy shopping and keep acquainted with new comings in the market.

5.4. Compare and Contrast Essay (example two)

The second essay example is about similarities and differences between crocodiles and alligators. The first step in writing is brainstorming, which is done here via Venn diagram. Major points to discuss in this essay are presented in diagram 3.

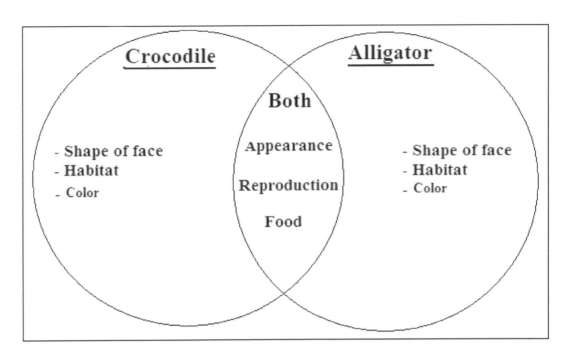

Diagram 3, differences and similarities between crocodiles and alligators

The information in diagram 3 is broadened in more details in table 8.

Crocodile	Both	Alligator
- Jaws: narrow snout, protruding back teeth in lower jaw - habitat: tropical areas in Africa, Asia, Australia, South America - Color: tan, olive	- Appearance: : large, scary - Reproduction: lay eggs - Food: eat mammals	- Jaws: broad snout, back teeth in lower jaw not showing - habitat: freshwater in North America and China - Color: blackish grey

Table 8, differences and similarities between crocodiles and alligators

The next step is to build a thesis. Here is one suggestion:

Crocodiles and alligators may look alike; however, there are differences between them.

After that, an outline is structured. The following are example outlines for the block and point-by-point styles.

Block Outline:

I. Introduction

   a. General review

   b. Thesis (Crocodiles and alligators, though may look alike, have differences between them).

II. Body

    a. Topic sentence (Similarities between crocodiles and alligators).

    i. Supporting detail # 1

        1.   Appearance

    ii. Supporting detail # 2

        1.   Reproduction.

    iii. Supporting detail # 3

        1.   Food.

    b. Topic sentence (Differences between crocodiles and alligators).

    i. Supporting detail # 1 (Jaws).

        1.   Crocodiles (snout, teeth).

        2.   Alligators (snout, teeth).

    ii. Supporting detail # 2 (Habitat).

        1.   Crocodiles (tropical areas)

        2.   Alligators (freshwater).

    iii. Supporting detail # 2

        1.   Crocodiles (tan, olive).

        2.   Alligator (blackish grey).

III. Conclusion

    a. Thesis restatement.

    b. General review.

Point-by-point Outline

I. Introduction

    a. General Review.

    b. Thesis (Crocodiles and alligators, though may look alike, have differences between them).

II. Body

    a. Topic sentence (similarity # 1).

    i. Supporting detail # 1 Appearance.

    b. Topic sentence (similarity # 2).

ii. Supporting detail # 2 Reproduction.

c. Topic sentence (similarity # 3).

iii. Supporting detail # 1 Food.

d. Topic sentence (difference #1). (Jaws).

i. Crocodile (snout, teeth).

ii. Alligator (snout, teeth).

e. Topic sentence (difference # 2) (Habitat).

i. Crocodile (tropical areas).

ii. Alligator (freshwater).

f. Topic sentence (difference # 3) (Color).

i. Crocodile (tan, olive).

ii. Alligator (blackish grey).

III. Conclusion

a. Thesis restatement.

b. General review

Below are the essay styles about the topic (differences and similarities between crocodiles and alligators).

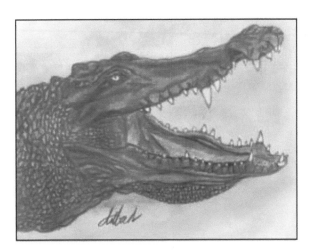

Block Essay

We are all familiar with the expressions 'after a while crocodile!', and 'see you later alligator!' Some people use the words "crocodile" and "alligator" to refer to the same creature which looks like a giant lizard with big pointed teeth and swims in the water. Crocodiles and alligators are scaly-skinned, cold-blooded reptiles that need to live in a warm climate because their body temperature cannot adjust with cold weather. These reptiles share many characteristics which cause confusion to some people telling them apart. Crocodiles and alligators, though may look alike, have differences between them.

Both crocodiles and alligators are large, scary reptiles with pointed teeth and long tails which are used for swimming by sweeping them from side to side. In addition, the bodies of crocodiles as well as alligators are adapted to live in their natural habitat as reptiles. For example, the position of their eyes and nostrils on the top of their heads allows them to breathe while swimming by keeping their heads out of the water. Furthermore, their eyes are covered with transparent skin layers that enable them to see when they are under the water. A second similarity between crocodiles and alligators is their reproduction system. Both reptiles and crocodiles lay eggs and cover them with sand and/or piles of plant material. Once the babies hatch, they head straight to water with the help of their mothers who carry them in their mouths or sometimes on their backs. Baby crocodiles and alligators feed on snails and small insects until they grow up and start hunting mammals. This leads us to the final similarity between crocodiles and alligators. Both reptiles hunt mammals for food by using their strong tails and powerful jaws. Despite the fact that these reptiles have the ability to catch big mammals such as cattle, their teeth are not strong enough to tear the prey apart and chew it. Instead, they shake it around in their mouths until they tear it off into big pieces of meat and swallow them as whole chunks.

With these similarities between crocodiles and alligators, differences exist. One difference is related to their jaws. Crocodiles have narrow pointed triangular snouts with their back teeth in the two jaws become visible when they close their mouths. In contrast, alligators have broad blunt snouts that are shaped like the letter U. In addition, their back teeth cannot be seen when the mouth is closed because they fit into small sockets which exist in the upper jaw. Another difference that holds between these two reptiles is their natural habitats. While crocodiles can live in salty water, alligators cannot. The reason is the difference of the functions these reptile's glands do. Crocodiles' glands can filter out excess salt from their bodies; alligators' glands cannot and therefore can only live in fresh water. Crocodiles are found in Africa, Asia, Australia, and South America, whereas alligators live in North American and China. A last difference is the colors of these reptiles. Crocodiles have light tan, olive colors while alligators are dark blackish grey and can be dark green depending on the quality of water they swim in. For example, the more the algae in the water, the greener the alligator's skin becomes.

As we can see, crocodiles and alligators are different even though they seem to be very similar. They lay eggs, eat mammal, and share general similar appearance with different details in the shape of the face. Also, they live in different natural habitats and have different colors. Despite the differences, everybody knows that these reptiles are dangerous predators that we should stay away from.

Point-by-point Essay

We are all familiar with the expressions "after a while crocodile!", and "see you later alligator"! Some people use the words "crocodile" and "alligator" to refer to the same creature which looks like a giant lizard with big pointed teeth and swims in the water. Crocodiles and alligators are scaly-skinned, cold-blooded reptiles that need to live in a warm climate because their body temperature cannot adjust with cold weather. These reptiles share many characteristics which cause confusion to some people telling them apart. Crocodiles and alligators, though may look alike, have differences between them.

Both crocodiles and alligators are large, scary reptiles with pointed teeth and long tails which are used for swimming by sweeping them from side to side. In addition, the bodies of crocodiles as well as alligators are adapted to live in their natural habitat as reptiles. For example, the position of their eyes and nostrils on the top of their heads allows them to breathe while swimming by keeping their heads out of the water. Furthermore, their eyes are covered with transparent skin layers that enable them to see when they are under the water.

A second similarity between crocodiles and alligators is their reproduction system. Both reptiles and crocodiles lay eggs and cover them with sand and/or piles of plant material. Once the babies hatch, they head straight to water with the help of their mothers who carry them in their mouths or sometimes on their backs. Baby crocodiles and alligators feed on snails and small insects until they grow up and start hunting mammals.

This leads us to the final similarity between crocodiles and alligators. Both reptiles hunt mammals for food by using their strong tails and powerful jaws. Despite the fact that these reptiles have the ability to catch big mammals such as cattle, their teeth are not strong enough to tear the prey apart and chew it. Instead, they shake it around in their mouths until they tear it off into big pieces of meat and swallow them as whole chunks.

With these similarities between crocodiles and alligators, differences exist. One difference is related to their jaws. Crocodiles have narrow pointed triangular snouts with their back teeth in the two jaws become visible when they close their mouths. In contrast, alligators have broad blunt snouts that are shaped like the letter U. In addition, their back teeth cannot be seen when the mouth is closed because they fit into small sockets which exist in the upper jaw.

Another difference that holds between these two reptiles is their natural habitats. While crocodiles can live in salty water, alligators cannot. The reason is the difference of the functions these reptile's glands do. Crocodiles' glands can filter out excess salt from their bodies; alligators' glands cannot and therefore can only live in fresh water. Crocodiles are found in Africa, Asia, Australia, and South America, whereas alligators live in North American and China.

A last difference is the colors of these reptiles. Crocodiles have light tan, olive colors while alligators are dark blackish grey and can be dark green depending on the quality of water they swim in. For example, the more the algae in the water, the greener the alligator's skin becomes.

As we can see, crocodiles and alligators are different even though they seem to be very similar. They lay eggs, eat mammal, and share general similar appearance with different details in the shape of the face. Also, they live in different natural habitats and have different colors. Despite the differences, everybody knows that these reptiles are dangerous predators that we should stay away from.

5.5. Compare and Contrast Essay (example three)

One other way to write a compare and contrast essay is to generate the outline from paragraphs or other essays. The next essay sample includes a comparison and a contrast between two individuals based on information about the two of them provided in two separate paragraphs. Paragraph A is about Waleed, and paragraph B is about Abdulmalik.

A. Waleed   B. Abdulmalik

A.   I have dreams that need patience and effort in order for them to come true. My name is Waleed and I am a reporter, a photographer and an editor in more than one local newspaper and journal in Misrata. I have a diploma in computer science, and now I study general management. I have a great passion in reading and sports, especially soccer. Since I am the photographer and editor in a sports Journal, I take pleasure in addition to responsibility in documenting soccer games and interview the players. I may not have achieved all of the goals I have set to accomplish; however, I still work hard to make the best future I can have in my career and life in general. Currently, I am preparing for a new business of my own that I hope I gain success in and contribute to the economic development of my city. Life has taught me that there is no end to dreams; once one is fulfilled, a new one emerges and finds its way in your list of future goals. Dreams are the key factor that keeps us going and moving towards a better life.

B.   My name is Abdulmalik. I have always had dreams that motivate me to move forward in order to achieve my goals. I have a Bachelor degree in Oil Engineering from Misrata University. After working as an engineer for a period of time, I have chosen a different path for my professional career and decided to become a reporter. At the present time, I work as a reporter, a correspondent to a news channel and a news writer. I have taken courses and workshops in media in different counties and have obtained many certificates. One of the main reasons why I love being a reporter is because it gives me the chance not just to watch my favorite soccer team play, but also to interview the player and the coach and learn more about their lives and career. My biggest desire is to become a well-known successful and respectful reporter who can be an active member in the society. I am aware that achieving this goal is full of challenges and obstacles; however, I know that hard work always pays off eventually, and I am positive I will enjoy success in my career and life.

The information provided about Waleed and Abdulmalik is organized in table 9 in terms of the things they have in common and the things in which they differ.

Waleed	Both	Abdulmalik
- Computer science	- desire to fulfill dreams	- Oil engineer
- Photographer, editor	- Hard work for better future	- Correspondent in news channel
- A new business	- Reporter	- Famous reporter
	- Passion for soccer	

Table 9, differences and similarities between Waleed and Abdulmalik

Next, the thesis statement is formed, as follows:

Waleed and Abdulmalik, despite of the common orientations they share, have their own differences.

Now the outline is formed based on the two types of compare and contrast essay styles.

Block Outline:

I.   Introduction

a.   General review

b.   Thesis (Waleed and Abdulmalik, despite of the common orientations they share, have their own differences).

II.   Body

a.   Topic sentence (Similarities between Waleed and Abdulmalik).

i. Supporting detail # 1

1. Desire to fulfill dreams

ii. Supporting detail # 2

1.   Hard work

iii. Supporting detail # 3

1.   Reporter

iv. Supporting detail # 4

1. Passion for soccer

b.   Topic sentence (Differences between Waleed and Abdulmalik).

i. Supporting detail # 1 (education).

1.   Waleed (computer science).

2.   Abdulmalik (oil engineer).

ii. Supporting detail # 2 (job).

1.   Waleed (photographer, editor)

2.   Abdulmalik (correspondent, news writer).

i.   Supporting detail # 3 (future plans)

1.   Waleed (new business).

2.   Abdulmalik (famous reporter).

III. Conclusion

a.   Thesis restatement.

b.   General review.

Point-by-point Outline

I. Introduction

    a. General Review.

    b. Thesis (Waleed and Abdulmalik, despite of the common orientations they share, have their own differences).

II. Body

    a. Topic sentence (similarity # 1).

        1. Supporting detail # 1 desire to fulfill dreams.

    b. Topic sentence (similarity # 2).

        1.   Supporting detail # 2 hard work.

    c. Topic sentence (similarity # 3).

        1. Supporting detail # 3 reporter

    d. Topic sentence (similarity # 4).

        1.   Supporting detail # 1 Passion for soccer.

    e. Topic sentence (difference # 1) (education).

        1.   Waleed (computer science)

        2.   Abdulmalik (oil engineer)

    f. Topic sentence (difference # 2) (job)

        1.   Waleed (photographer, editor).

        2.   Abdulmalik (correspondent, news writer).

    g. Topic sentence (difference # 3) (future plans).

        1. Waleed (new business).

        2. Abdulmalik (famous reporter)

III. Conclusion

    a. Thesis restatement.

    b. General review

The following is the whole essay in two styles.

The Block Essay

Fulfilling the dreams is the utmost goal for every individual and it is the big motive to persistence and perseverance. Everybody wishes for development and improvement both at the personal and professional levels. Having a better life requires hard work and strong will in addition to the insistence to keep trying and never give up. Waleed and Abdulmalik are two young gentlemen who have goals that they work to accomplish and improve the quality of their lives. Waleed and Abdulmalik, despite of the common orientations they share, have their own differences.

Among the similarities Waleed and Abdulmalik have is their ambition for improvement. Both gentlemen are hard-working individuals who seek better lives by choosing the jobs they have interest in and they can do best. Waleed and Abdulmalik have more than one job that they do with pleasure and enjoyment. The two gentlemen are determined to obtain a better future and better quality of life. In addition, they both like to keep trying and never give up, to always have a dream to fulfill and to constantly improve their careers and lives. Moreover, they are ready to change jobs and challenge their potentials. This results in the second similarity between the two of them. Both Waleed and Abdulmalik are reporters. After graduating from different fields of specialty, they both work as reporters and dedicate themselves to their jobs. They have multiple jobs at a time and they challenge themselves to succeed and reach to their goals. A last point in the similarities is that in addition to their desire to accomplish their goals, the two gentlemen like to have jobs in which they can enjoy their hobbies. They both share a passion in soccer and they love documenting reports about soccer events and interviewing the players. Doing a job they love exaggerates their determination to become successful and overcome obstacles.

In addition to these similarities, differences do exist. The first difference between Walled and Abdulmalik is education. Walled has a diploma in computer science and is currently studying general management. On the other hand, Abdulmalik has a bachelor degree in oil engineering; nevertheless, both have chosen careers that are not related to their fields of specialty and decided to work as reporters among other things. Besides being reporters, Waleed and Abdulmalik have other different jobs. While Waleed works as a photographer and an editor in a newspaper and a journal, Abdulmalik is a correspondent to a news channel and a news writer in addition to the courses he takes in media to keep himself professional and updated in his career. Furthermore, having different plans for the future is another distinction between Waleed and Abdulmalik. Waleed has a goal to start a business on his own and be successful in it to help developing the economy of his city. Abdulmalik, on the other hand, desires to perpetuate his career in media and desires to become a famous and successful reporter who can make a difference in his society.

With the differences that hold between Waleed and Abdulmalik in their careers, they are similar to some extent. Both of them have big dreams and make great efforts to achieve their goals to participate in developing their community. The two gentlemen believe in hard work in order to expand self-esteem required to build up the individual's personal and professional identities and the feeling of belonging and fulfillment.

The Point-by- Point Essay

Fulfilling the dreams is the utmost goal for every individual and it is the big motive to persistence and perseverance. Everybody wishes for development and improvement both at the personal and professional levels. Having a better life requires hard work and strong will in addition to the insistence to keep trying and never give up. Waleed and Abdulmalik are two young gentlemen who have goals that they work to accomplish and improve the quality of their lives. Waleed and Abdulmalik, despite of the common orientations they share, have their own differences.

Among the similarities Waleed and Abdulmalik have is their ambition for improvement. Both gentlemen are hard-working individuals who seek better lives by choosing the jobs they have interest in and they can do best. Waleed and Abdulmalik have more than one job that they do with pleasure and enjoyment.

The two gentlemen are determined to obtain a better future and better quality of life. In addition, they both like to keep trying and never give up, to always have a dream to fulfill and to constantly improve their careers and lives. Moreover, they are ready to change jobs and challenge their potentials.

This results in the second similarity between the two of them. Both Waleed and Abdulmalik are reporters. After graduating from different fields of specialty, they both work as reporters and dedicate themselves to their jobs. They have multiple jobs at a time and they challenge themselves to succeed and reach to their goals.

A last point in the similarities is that in addition to their desire to accomplish their goals, the two gentlemen like to have jobs in which they can enjoy their hobbies. They both share a passion in soccer and they love documenting reports about soccer events and interviewing the players. Doing a job they love exaggerates their determination to become successful and overcome obstacles.

In addition to these similarities, differences do exist. The first difference between Walled and Abdulmalik is education. Walled has a diploma in computer science and is currently studying general management. On the other hand, Abdulmalik has a bachelor degree in oil engineering; nevertheless, both have chosen careers that are not related to their fields of specialty and decided to work as reporters among other things.

Besides being reporters, Waleed and Abdulmalik have other different jobs. While Waleed works as a photographer and an editor in a newspaper and a journal, Abdulmalik is a correspondent to a news channel and a news writer in addition to the courses he takes in media to keep himself professional and updated in his career.

Furthermore, having different plans for the future is another distinction between Waleed and Abdulmalik. Waleed has a goal to start a business on his own and be successful in it to help developing the economy of his city. Abdulmalik, on the other hand, desires to perpetuate his career in media and desires to become a famous and successful reporter who can make a difference in his society.

With the differences that hold between Waleed and Abdulmalik in their careers, they are similar to some extent. Both of them have big dreams and make great efforts to achieve their goals to participate in developing their community. The two gentlemen believe in hard work in order to expand self-esteem required to build up the individual's personal and professional identities and the feeling of belonging and fulfillment.

5. 6. Compare and Contrast Essay (example four)

One kind of compare and contrast essay is used to discuss the similarities and differences between stories or events presented in two different kinds of media. For example, similarities and differences can be found in the characters and/ or events of a novel and a movie. Whether the movie is based on the novel to which it is compared or on a different one, there are always aspects which are different and aspects that they have in common. The first thing to do is to write a comprehensive summary of each plot and then classify the aspects of similarity and difference in a Venn diagram or a table before working on the essay.

The following is an example essay that compares and contrasts events and characters of a novel and a movie. First, a summary for each plot is provided.

-   Novel: *HATCHET* (1987) by Gary Paulsen.
-   Movie: *CAST AWAY* (2000) Director: Robert Zemeckis. Screenplay: William Broyles Jr.

Summary of *Hatchet*

A thirteen-year-old boy named Brian Robeson flies on a small bush plane from New York City to the oil fields located in Canada to spend the summer with his father after his parent's divorce. During the flight, the pilot shows Brian how to hold the paddles and lets him fly the plane for a while. But after that the pilot has a heart attack all of a sudden and passes away. Brian has no other alternative but to manage the plane and try to land it as safely as he possibly can. He fails to get the signal on the radio to ask for help. The plane crashes into an L-shaped lake in the middle of the Canadian forest and Brian survives the crash.

Brian manages to leave the plane with few bruises and the hatchet, a gift from his mother, attached to his belt. He cannot take anything from the plane because it drowns to the bottom of the lake. Still devastated from the divorce of his parents due to his mother's involvement with another man, Brian realizes that he needs to forget about his sadness over his family issues and find a way to survive in the Canadian wilderness and endure his new stressful life until he is rescued. With the help of the hatchet, Brian makes a shelter by cutting some tree branches and using them to cover an underside of a big rock overhanging like a cave. He also finds some berries to silence his hunger. Nevertheless, Brian knows that he needs to learn how to make a fire, how to fish, and how to hunt animals for food.

Brian succeeds to make a fire by collecting little sticks and piling them in a small fire pit. Then he takes his hatchet and strongly hits it on the side of his shelter rock to generate sparks that ignite the sticks and create fire. Brian has to eat raw turtle eggs and make a bow and an arrow with his hatchet and finds a way to learn fishing and hunting. He also needs to figure out how to keep his shelter and himself protected from wild animals such as a skunk, a porcupine, and even a moose that attack him on his search for food.

While Brian struggles to survive in these severe conditions, a tornado hits the forest and destroys the shelter he has made. But fortunately, the tornado also causes the water in the lake to churn and bring the crashed plane up to the surface. Brian uses his hatchet to make a hole to the side of the plane to get into it. Inside the plane, Brian finds an emergency survival pack that belongs to the dead pilot. He opens the pack and finds many useful items such as a sleeping bag, lighters, cooking equipment, frozen food packs, a compass, medical kit, a rifle and an emergency transmitter. Brian flips the switch on the transmitter a few times but hears nothing. For a while, he thinks that the transmitter is broken due to the plane crash. However, after a short time a plane suddenly appears and lands on the lake. The pilot steps out of it and tells Brain that he has picked up the signal from the transmitter. Brian is rescued after being stranded in the wilderness for about three months and is finally sent back to his mother.

Summary of *Cast Away*

Chuck Noland works as a Federal Express engineer whose job requires him to travel most of the time. He keeps putting off marriage from his girlfriend, Kelly, because of the busy schedules the two of them have. In fact, Chuck's schedule is so busy that he has to exchange Christmas gifts with his girlfriend on the car in his way to airport where he travels for work. She gives him a pocket watch with her picture in it and he gives her an engagement ring. Chuck proposes to Kelly and goes for his business trip to deliver packages. During the trip, the plane suddenly crashes into the Pacific Ocean due to technical difficulties and Chuck fastens his seat belt and waits until the plane hits the water to get on the life boat. He wakes up the next morning to find himself stranded on an isolated island away from any human contact. The first thing Chuck does is collecting tree truck to make the word HELP on the sand in order to be hopefully seen from a plane. Chuck knows that help may not come soon and therefore decides to adjust to his new emotionally, mentally and physically stressful life. The waves wash up some of the packages to the shore.

As one way to survive on the island, Chuck opens the packages and makes use of whatever he can find in them, except for one package that he leaves unopened throughout the four years he spends on the island. One day in one of his many attempts to make fire, he accidently cuts himself badly in the hand. With his blooded hand, he hits the volleyball he found in one of the packages very hardly because of the pain. The blood leaves tracks of his hand on the volleyball, and Chuck adds eyes and nose and mouth to the blood spot to make it look like a face. He becomes so attached to the face on the volleyball and starts treating it like a person and gives it the name Wilson. Chuck struggles through many obstacles while trying to find food, water, and make fire. Chuck has to rub a stick to a piece of bamboo many times until smoke comes out and he blows on it to make fire.

Chuck looks at the picture of Kelly in his pocket watch all the time to give him hope that he will be rescued. He lives on the island for four years during which he becomes skillful in making fire and catching fish with a spear. During his stay on the island, Chuck becomes overwhelmed with different feelings. He becomes furious when he fails to make fire, then he gets so excited after he manages to create it. Chuck finally decides to make a raft and leave the island to go to civilization. During the trip on the raft, Chuck wakes up from sleep to find a big ship sailing nearby. He is rescued at last. He returns home to find his girlfriend married and has her own family. He takes the package that he never opens during his stay on the island and delivers it to the address where a young lady lives.

After providing the summaries of the two stories, the second step to take is to classify the differences and similarities between these stories in table 10.

Hatchet	Both	Cast Away
- A young boy visiting his father. - Pilot dies, plane crashes in a forest. - Endurance: manages to land the plane on the lake, stays sane, and talked to no one, attacked by animals. - Creation of fire with hatchet - Stayed in the forest and rescued by a plane	- Isolation and struggle - Survival and adjustment - Shelter/ food/ fire	- A grown-up FedEx worker. - Technical difficulty, plane crashes near island. - Endurance: stays still in the plane, overwhelmed with feelings, and talked to Wilson, no animal attack. Creation of fire with sticks - Left the island and rescued by a ship

Table 10, Differences and similarities between Hatchet and Cast Away

After organizing the information in table 10, the thesis for the compare and contrast essay is structured. As follows

Although Hatchet and Cast Away share the major story of surviving in standard isolation, they have their own differences in some details.

Now comes the outline step. Below is the outline in the two styles.

Block Outline:

I.   Introduction

    a.   General review

    b.   Thesis (Although Hatchet and Cast Away share the major story of surviving in standard isolation, they have their own differences in some details).

II. Body

    a. Topic sentence (Similarities).

i. Supporting detail # 1

    1. Isolation and struggle

ii. Supporting detail # 2

    1.   Survival and adjustment

b. Topic sentence (Differences).

i. Supporting detail # 1 (main characters).

    1.   Hatchet (young boy).

    2.   Cast Away (Adult man).

ii. Supporting detail # 2 (plane crash).

    1.   Hatchet (pilot dies)

    2.   Cast away (Technical difficulty).

iii. Supporting detail # 3 (Endurance)

    1.   Hatchet (stays sane, talks to no one, attacked by animals).

    2.   Cast Away (overwhelmed with feelings, talks to volleyball, not attacked).

iv. Supporting detail # 4 (fire)

    1.   Hatchet (create fire with hatchet)

    2.   Cast Away (create fire with sticks)

v. Supporting detail # 5 (rescue)

    1. Hatchet (plane receives signal).

    2. Cast Away (build a raft and found by a ship).

I.   Conclusion

    a. Thesis restatement.

    b. General review.

Point-by-point Outline

    I. Introduction

        a.   General Review.

        b.   Thesis (Although Hatchet and Cast Away share the major story of surviving in standard isolation, they have their own differences in some details).

    II. Body

    a. Topic sentence (similarity # 1)

       1. Supporting detail # 1 isolation and struggle.

  b. Topic sentence (similarity # 2)

       1. Supporting detail # 2 survival and assessment

  c. Topic sentence (difference # 1) (main characters)

       1.   Hatchet (young boy)

       2.   Cast Away (adult man)

  d. Topic sentence (difference # 2) (plane crash)

       1.   Hatchet (pilot dies)

       2.   Cast Away (Technical difficulty)

  e. Topic sentence (difference # 3) (Endurance)

       1. Hatchet (stays sane, talks to no one, attacked by animals)

       2. Cast Away (overwhelmed with feelings, talks to volleyball, not attacked)

  f. Topic sentence (difference # 4) (fire)

       1. Hatchet (create fire with hatchet)

       2. Cast Away (create fire with sticks)

  g. Topic sentence (difference # 5) (rescue)

       1. Hatchet (plane receives signal)

       2. Cast Away (build a raft and found by a ship)

III.   Conclusion

  a. Thesis restatement.

  b. General review

The Block Essay

Surviving extreme conditions is as old as ice age. Humans have the ability to adapt to new conditions and find ways to adjust to a new life. When bad incidents happen, they cause a big shock at first resulting in negative effects at the emotional and physical levels. Nevertheless, humans manage to pounce back to their senses in order to survive. The novel Hatchet (1987) by Gary Paulsen, and the movie Cast Away (2000) directed by Robert Zemeckis deal with surviving isolation, departure from civilization, and scarcity of basic needs that humans take for granted. Although Hatchet and Cast Away share the major story of surviving in standard isolation, they have their own differences in some details.

Isolation and struggle are common features between Hatchet and Cast Away. Both characters find themselves in isolated places completely disconnected from any kind of human civilization, and they have to survive while deprived from their basic needs. Moreover, the new life causes stress and pressure that have an impact on the characters' mental, emotional, and physical status. This is possibly increased in relation to the family issues the two characters have to deal with. The character in Hatchet, Brian, is going through an uneasy time dealing with the divorce of his parents, while the character in Cast Away, Chuck, cannot find time in his busy schedule to propose to his girlfriend. The two characters prepare to have a new life even before the plane crash incident takes place. The life Brian and Chuck go through after the plane crash is another similarity. The two characters are pushed to the breaking point in order to survive the extreme conditions in their isolation. The basic life they used to take for granted is no longer available for them. Food is no longer within the reach of their hands; they need to go search for it every time they are hungry. Additionally, they have to use tools to hunt animals and catch fish to eat them. This means that they need to make a fire to cook the food. Likewise, Brian and Chuck need to protect themselves and have some kind of home to return to at the end of the day.

Even though the two characters share many aspects, they are not the same in many others. The first difference is the characters themselves. In Hatchet, Brian is a thirteen-year-old boy who is flying from New York to spend the summer with his father who works in an oil field in Canada. On the other hand, Chuck, in Cast Away, is an adult man who works in FedEx Company and whose job requires constant travel even on holidays, making it difficult for him to marry his girlfriend. A second difference between the survival stories of Brian and Chuck is the plane crash incident. In Hatchet, the pilot suddenly has a heart attack and dies on the air and the plane crashes in the Canadian wilderness, whereas in Cast Away, a technical difficulty causes the crash of the plane into the Pacific Ocean. Although the two incidents are naturally scary and cause the feeling of confusion and helplessness at least temporarily, the two characters have different reactions in this situation. These reactions are the focus of the third point of difference between Brian and Chuck; i.e. endurance. Brian, despite his young age, stays calm during the plane crash and holds the controls of the plane as an attempt to land safely. In contrast, Chuck fastens his seatbelt and does nothing as he fearfully watches the plane goes down. There are two possible reasons for the behavior of the two characters. The first one is that in the pilot in Hatchet gives Brian general instructions on how to fly the plane and lets him fly it for a while. Chuck, on the other hand, does not get this chance. Also, Brian is the only one on the plane with the pilot so he knows by nature that landing the plane is his direct responsibility after the death of the pilot. Contrary to this, Chuck is with FedEx team with a pilot and a copilot who both stay alive during the plane crash. Similar features of endurance are also observed in the two characters' behavior in their new isolated locations. Brian stays relatively sane most of the time even though he does not talk to anyone and he is occasionally attacked by wild animals. In a different manner, Chuck expresses overwhelming feelings towards almost everything that happens to him. He breaks into tears when he sees one of the men who were with him on the plane dead at the island's beach. Furthermore, he creates a face from the big blood spot he stains the volleyball with and makes it a friend that he calls Wilson. He talks to Wilson all the time and shares stories with him. He even cries loudly and burst into tears when he loses Wilson in the middle of the ocean when he leaves the island. Unlike Brian who does not show big excitement after making a fire, Chuck becomes so excited when he creates the fire and gives loud screams of joy and triumph to express his happiness towards this achievement. Making a fire represents another difference in the story. Brian uses his hatchet to cause sparks to ignite the sticks and create a fire. This is not the same with Chuck who has to rub a stick to a piece of bamboo stick to create a fire. Chuck works hard to make a fire and needs to be patient as he keeps trying. He even wounds himself during the process unlike Brian who does not experience such trouble when he creates the fire. A final distinction between the stories of Brian and Chuck is their rescue. When the tornado hits the forest where Brian is located, it brings the plane up to the surface of the lake, and Brian manages to get the supplies out of the plane. Differently, Chuck builds a raft to leave the island. It is possible that after Brian finds the supplies in the plane, he restores comfort and preparedness to live in the forest for a longer period of time. While Chuck's rescue is purposeful and intended from his part, Brian's rescue happens accidently after he sends a signal via the emergency transmitter he finds with the supplies.

Brian and Chuck, although they go through similar conditions in their attempts to survive and adjust, they react in different ways from each other. Surviving severe conditions is not impossible, yet it requires time, effort, and patience. In addition, it is stressful and painful and results in negative energy. It takes strong will and desire for humans to make it through these situations, and humans always end up finding a way to accomplish that.

The Point-by-point Essay

Surviving extreme conditions is as old as ice age. Humans have the ability to adapt to new conditions and find ways to adjust to a new life. When bad incidents happen, they cause a big shock at first resulting in negative effects at the emotional and physical levels. Nevertheless, humans manage to pounce back to their senses in order to survive. The novel Hatchet (1987) by Gary Paulsen, and the movie Cast Away (2000) directed by Robert Zemeckis deal with surviving isolation, departure from civilization, and scarcity of basic needs that humans take for granted. Although Hatchet and Cast Away share the major story of surviving in standard isolation, they have their own differences in some details.

Isolation and struggle are common features between Hatchet and Cast Away. Both characters find themselves in isolated places completely disconnected from any kind of human civilization, and they have to survive while deprived from their basic needs. Moreover, the new life causes stress and pressure that have an impact on the characters' mental, emotional, and physical status. This is possibly increased in relation to the family issues the two characters have to deal with. The character in Hatchet, Brian, is going through an uneasy time dealing with the divorce of his parents, while the character in Cast Away, Chuck, cannot find time in his busy schedule to propose to his girlfriend. The two characters prepare to have a new life even before the plane crash incident takes place.

The life Brian and Chuck go through after the plane crash is another similarity. The two characters are pushed to the breaking point in order to survive the extreme conditions in their isolation. The basic life they used to take for granted is no longer available for them. Food is no longer within the reach of their hands; they need to go search for it every time they are hungry. Additionally, they have to use tools to hunt animals and catch fish to eat them. This means that they need to make a fire to cook the food. Likewise, Brian and Chuck need to protect themselves and have some kind of home to return to at the end of the day.

Even though the two characters share many aspects, they are not the same in many others. The first difference is the characters themselves. In Hatchet, Brian is a thirteen-year-old boy who is flying from New York to spend the summer with his father who works in an oil field in Canada. On the other hand, Chuck, in Cast Away, is an adult man who works in FedEx Company and whose job requires constant travel even on holidays, making it difficult for him to marry his girlfriend.

A second difference between the survival stories of Brian and Chuck is the plane crash incident. In Hatchet, the pilot suddenly has a heart attack and dies on the air and the plane crashes in the Canadian wilderness, whereas in Cast Away, a technical difficulty causes the crash of the plane into the Pacific Ocean. Although the two incidents are naturally scary and cause the feeling of confusion and helplessness at least temporarily, the two characters have different reactions in this situation.

These reactions are the focus of the third point of difference between Brian and Chuck; i.e. endurance. Brian, despite his young age, stays calm during the plane crash and holds the controls of the plane as an attempt to land safely. In contrast, Chuck fastens his seatbelt and does nothing as he fearfully watches the plane goes down. There are two possible reasons for the behavior of the two characters. The first one is that in the pilot in Hatchet gives Brian general instructions on how to fly the plane and lets him fly it for a while. Chuck, on the other hand, does not get this chance. Also, Brian is the only one on the plane with the pilot so he knows by nature that landing the plane is his direct responsibility after the death of the pilot. Contrary to this, Chuck is with FedEx team with a pilot and a copilot who both stay alive during the plane crash. Similar features of endurance are also observed in the two characters' behavior in their new isolated locations. Brian stays relatively sane most of the time even though he does not talk to anyone and he is occasionally attacked by wild animals. In a different manner, Chuck expresses overwhelming feelings towards almost everything that happens to him. He breaks into tears when he sees one of the men who were with him on the plane dead at the island's beach. Furthermore, he creates a face from the big blood spot he stains the volleyball with and makes it a friend that he calls Wilson. He talks to Wilson all the time and shares stories with him. He even cries loudly and burst into tears when he loses Wilson in the middle of the ocean when he leaves the island. Unlike Brian who does not show big excitement after making a fire, Chuck becomes so excited when he creates the fire and gives loud screams of joy and triumph to express his happiness towards this achievement.

Making a fire represents another difference in the story. Brian uses his hatchet to cause sparks to ignite the sticks and create a fire. This is not the same with Chuck who has to rub a stick to a piece of bamboo stick to create a fire. Chuck works hard to make a fire and needs to be patient as he keeps trying. He even wounds himself during the process unlike Brian who does not experience such trouble when he creates the fire.

A final distinction between the stories of Brian and Chuck is their rescue. When the tornado hits the forest where Brian is located, it brings the plane up to the surface of the lake, and Brian manages to get the supplies out of the plane. Differently, Chuck builds a raft to leave the island. It is possible that after Brian finds the supplies in the plane, he restores comfort and preparedness to live in the forest for a longer period of time. While Chuck's rescue is purposeful and intended from his part, Brian's rescue happens accidently after he sends a signal via the emergency transmitter he finds with the supplies.

Brian and Chuck, although they go through similar conditions in their attempts to survive and adjust, they react in different ways from each other. Surviving severe conditions is not impossible, yet it requires time, effort, and patience. In addition, it is stressful and painful and results in negative energy. It takes strong will and desire for humans to make it through these situations, and humans always end up finding a way to accomplish that.

5.7. Compare and Contrast Essay (example five)

This example presents a compare and contrast essay example about a novel and a movie based on the story in that novel. The essay focuses on points of similarities and differences between the two plots. The chosen story is the following:

- The Five People You Meet in Heaven (2003) by Mitch Albom.
- The Five People You Meet in Heaven (2004) directed by Lloyd Kramer.

We first provide summaries for each one.

Summary of *The Five People You Meet in Heaven* novel (2003)

The story is about a retired veteran named Eddie who works in an amusement park. His job is maintaining the rides and making sure they function well. He makes animals from pipe cleaners to children, and he talks occasionally to Dominquez, a guy who works at the park who is getting ready to take his wife to Mexico where Eddie has never been. Eddie rides in every ride once a week to make sure it works properly. Eddie dies as he tries to save a little girl from getting crashed under one of the carts of the Freddy's Free Fall ride. The cart is tilted beneath the upper platform of the ride and people are freaked out. Edie sees Dominguez and Willie release the cart after getting everybody out of it. He tries to tell them not to cut the wire but they do not hear him. The cart comes loose and drops down fast so Eddie has to hurry to safe the girl; the cart hits him and he passes away.

Upon his death, Eddie meets five people that are connected to him somehow someway when he used to be alive. He comes to an understanding about life after he dies. After Eddie dies, he does not feel pain, he is happy. He sees himself at the beach and everything changes colors. Eddie remembers moments from his fifth birthday and how his mother was happy with him for being a good boy. He sees himself inside a large teacup at the amusement park, and he cannot find his cane to help him get up. He is healthy and can walk with no cane, and above all, Ruby Pier looks like what it was when he was a child not what it looks like now.

The first person Eddie meets is a man with a blue skin named Blue Man. Blue Man tells Eddie that he killed him. Blue Man was driving a car and tried not to hit the little boy Eddie who wanted to catch the ball. So Blue Man tried not to hit Eddie and as a result he lost control of his car and hit a parked truck. At that immediate moment, the Blue Man had a heart attack and died. Blue Man tells Eddie that all people are connected, and that death misses someone to take another. Eddie asks Blue Man if he has saved the little girl from the crashing cart at Ruby Pier, but Blue Man, who suddenly has a healthy pink skin, gives no answer. The novel keeps track of Eddie's birthdays and the events that took place in them. The colors of the sky change depending on how bad the memory is.

The second Person Eddie meets is his Captain, his Commanding Officer from war in Philippine. Eddie wanted to join the Army to prove to everybody that he is a strong man. Eddie practiced shooting at the shooting arcade at Ruby Pier. Eddie finds himself in the battle field, and he freaks out at the sight of his helmet with his name on it. Eddie tells the captain that he has not accomplished anything in his life, and that he has not seen any of his fellow soldiers after the war has ended. Eddie is captured with some friends by Philippine soldiers and are all forced to work in a coal mine. Eddie sleeps with Marguerite's picture propped up at his sight from his helmet. Eddie has a rough time during those days and has to watch one Philippine soldier killing his friend Robonzo because he is too sick to work. Eddie tries to find a way to escape the camp. He sees a Philippine soldier juggles stones and he seizes the opportunity being good at juggling. He offers to jog for the soldiers and then uses the stones to hit the soldiers and manages with his friends to kill the four soldiers and run out of their prison hut. Eddie and his friends burn up the whole camp before escaping in a vehicle their captain finds. As he burns the huts, Eddie sees a small figure inside the flames, he tries to inter the burning hut but he gets shot and his friends drag him away. As he talks with the Captain, Eddie learns that it is the Captain who shot him in the knee to stop him from entering the burning hut. Later, the captain shoots a gate open and walks in front of the vehicle to check the escape way for Eddie and soldiers. He steps on a mine and it explodes on him and he dies. The captain teaches Eddie the second lesson; sacrifice. The captain says he kept his word and never let his soldiers behind him. Eddie asks the Captain if he has saved that little girl from the falling cart in Ruby Pier, but the captain does not answer.

The third person Eddie meets is his father. Eddie finds himself in a outdoor diner in winter snow. He looks out of the window and sees his father. He has never had a good relationship with his father. He has never felt his love. His father slapped him and lashed him with the belt. There is negligence, violence, and silence.

Nevertheless, Eddie has admired his old man because this is human nature. Eddie's father always gives him maintenance work,and tells him to fix stuff. After the injury, Eddie stays at home and rarely talks to anybody. His father wants him to get a job and he gets violent but Eddie stops him. The book uses Eddie's birthdays to give updates of his life. After the war, Eddie works in a Taxi cab. When his father gets sick, Eddie has to work in Ruby Pier instead of his father in order to keep the job. Eddie never wanted to work in Ruby Pier; his dream job is to become an engineer. After he dies, Eddie meets with Ruby, an old woman whose name is used to name the amusement park. Ruby takes Eddie inside the diner and tells him about her husband, Emile, who has built Ruby Pier. She then draws a circle in the snow and Eddie watches inside it. He sees his father's best friend, Mickey getting drunk and goes inside his mother's bedroom and attacks her. He also sees his father entering and saving his mother, while Mickey runs out of the house and heads towards the ocean. Eddie's father follows Mickey who drops into the water. The father jumps after Mickey and saves him. Eddie does not understand why his father does that to somebody who attacks his wife. Ruby teaches Eddie the third lesson; forgiveness. Mickey has helped Eddie's father in the past to find a job and to provide for the family. At this point, Eddie remembers how he hates his father because he wants to be an engineer, he wants a better life but his father does not let him. Eddie does not earn much money, he does not leave anywhere. He blames it on his father for losing his freedom, his dream career and his hope. However, Eddie now learns to forgive and never holds to anger. He goes to his father at the diner and tells him that he forgives him. The father dies while bending over the ledge of the window of his hospital room in a very cold night.

The fourth person Eddie meets in heaven is Marguerite, his wife and the love of his life. Eddie finds himself in an empty room. He opens the door to a foreign wedding, German or Sweden. Then he coughs and everybody looks up so he leaves through the same door to find himself in a Spanish weeding. Then he coughs again and they look up and he leaves through the same door to find himself in an African wedding. At the Italian wedding, he sees Marguerite; she is the bride's maid. This makes him remember their small and simple wedding that took place in a small Chinese restaurant. Marguerite tells him she has met her five people already and this has helped her come to a better understanding of life. They both remember how they could not have a child of their own. Marguerite wants to adopt a child, but Eddie spends the money on horse race gambling. One day, Eddie calls Marguerite from the horse race and tells her he won, but she yells at him because they need to be more responsible for the adoption. Then she decides to drive to the horse ride to apologize for yelling at him on his birthday. She has a car accident and is sent to the hospital. The accident costs them the adoption because of the expenses and the delay. Also, she has brain tumor and this makes prevents them from talking about the child any more. Eddie tells Marguerite what happened after her death. He tells her that new rides are added in Ruby Pier; dangerous rides that Eddie does not like. She takes him into a room decorated like the hall where they had their wedding. They dance a little then she disappears.

The fifth and last person Eddie meets in heaven is a little girl. He hears sounds of children playing by the river. One little Asian girl waves to him with both hands, and he walks to her. She introduces herself to him, Tala. She points to each piece of her clothes and names it in her language. She says that she and the kids are washing in the river like their mothers used to do to them. He makes her a dog from pipe cleaners in his pocket as he used to do to children in Ruby Pier. The girl tells Eddie that he burned her. She was the shadow in that hut that he burned when he escaped his prison in Philippine. Eddie gets very sad and cries aloud and asks her to forgive him. She gives him a stone and asked him to wash her in the river. As he rubs the stone against her body, her skin gets healed from the burns. He tells her that he has accomplished nothing in his life, she says he keeps children at Ruby Pier save and happy. Eddie asks Tala about the little girl in the cart incident. She says he pushed her away and saved her. Tala says that it was her own hands that he grabbed, not the little girl's. She takes him to heaven to keep him safe. Tala takes him trough all colors to the ocean. When he gets out of the water, he finds himself in Ruby Pier crowded with so many people; he sees Marguerite and realizes he is finally home.

Summary of *The Five People You Meet in Heaven* Movie (2004)

The story is about a retired veteran named Eddie who works in an amusement park. His job is maintaining the rides and making sure they function well. He makes animals from pipe cleaners to children, and he talks occasionally to Dominquez, a guy who works at the park who is getting ready to take his wife to Miami where Eddie has never been. Eddie rides in every ride once a week to make sure it works properly. In addition to being skillful at fixing things, Eddie is also strong and fights for his older brother. Eddie dies as he tries to save a little girl from getting crashed under one of the carts of the Freddy's Free Fall ride. The cart is tilted beneath the upper platform of the ride and people are freaked out. The cart comes loose and drops down fast so Eddie has to hurry to safe the girl. The cart hits him and he passes away.

After his death, Eddie feels healthy and young. He is happy because does not feel the pain and he can run fast, but he cannot talk. He remembers when he was a child at the amusement park where his father used to take him to fix things. Eddie meets five people that are connected to him somehow someway when he used to be alive.

The first person Eddie meets is a man with a blue skin named Blue Man. Blue Man tells Eddie that he killed him. Blue Man was driving a car and tried not to hit the little boy Eddie who wanted to catch the ball. So Blue Man lost control of his car and hit a food stand. At that immediate moment, Blue Man had a heart attack and died. Blue Man tells Eddie that all people are connected, and that death misses someone to take another. Eddie asks Blue Man if he has saved the little girl from the crashing cart at Ruby Pier, but Blue Man, who suddenly has a healthy pink skin, gives no answer.

The second Person Eddie meets in heaven is his Captain, his Commanding Officer from war in Philippine. Eddie wanted to join the Army to prove to everybody that he is a strong man. Eddie practiced shooting at the shooting arcade at Ruby Pier. Eddie finds himself in the battle field, and he freaks out at the sight of his helmet with his name on it. Eddie tells the Captain that he has not accomplished anything in his life, and that he has not seen any of his fellow soldiers after the war has ended. Eddie is captured with some friends by Philippine soldiers and are all forced to work in a coal mine. Eddie sleeps with Marguerite's picture propped up at his sight from his helmet. Eddie has a rough time during those days and has to watch one Philippine soldier killing his friend Robonzo because he is too sick to work. Eddie tries to find a way to escape the camp. He sees a Philippine soldier juggles stones and he seizes the opportunity being good at juggling. He offers to jog for the soldiers and then uses the stones to hit the soldiers and manages with his friends to kill the four soldiers and run out of their prison hut. Eddie and his friends burn up the whole camp before escaping in a vehicle their captain finds. As he burns the huts, Eddie see a small figure inside the flames, he tries to inter the burning hut but he gets shot and his friends drag him away. As he talks with the Captain, Eddie learns that it is the Captain who shot him in the knee to stop him from entering the burning hut. Later, the captain shoots a gate open and walks in front of the vehicle to check the escape way for Eddie and soldiers. He steps on a mine and it explodes on him and he dies. The captain teaches Eddie the second lesson; sacrifice. The captain says he kept his word and never let his soldiers behind him. Eddie asks the Captain if he has saved that little girl from the falling cart in Ruby Pier, but the captain does not answer.

The third person Eddie meets is his father. Eddie finds himself in a outdoor diner in winter snow. He looks out of the window and sees his father. He has never had a good relationship with his father. He has never felt his love. His father slapped him and lashed him with the belt. There is negligence, violence, and silence. Nevertheless, Eddie has admired his old man because this is human nature. Eddie's father always gives him maintenance work and tells him to fix stuff. After the injury, Eddie stays at home and rarely talks to anybody. His father wants him to get a job and he gets violent but Eddie stops him. After the war, Eddie works in a Taxi cab. When his father gets sick, Eddie has to work in Ruby Pier instead of his father in order to keep the job. Eddie never wanted to work in Ruby Pier; his dream job is to become an engineer. After he dies, Eddie meets with Ruby, an old woman whose name is used to name the amusement park. Ruby takes Eddie inside the diner and tells him about her husband, Emile, who has built Ruby Pier. Then she takes Eddie inside the apartment where Eddie has grown up. He sees his father's best friend, Mickey getting drunk and goes inside his mother's bedroom and attacks her. He also sees his father entering and saving his mother, while Mickey runs out of the house and heads towards the ocean. Eddie's father follows Mickey who drops into the water. The father jumps after Mickey and saves him. Eddie does not understand why his father does that to somebody who attacks his wife. Ruby teaches Eddie the third lesson; forgiveness. Mickey has helped Eddie's father in the past to find a job and to provide for the family. At this point, Eddie remembers how he hates his father because he wants to be an engineer, he wants a better life but his father does not let him. Eddie does not earn much money, he does not leave anywhere. He blames it on his father for losing his freedom, his dream career and his hope. However, Eddie now learns to forgive and never holds to anger. He goes to his father at the diner, holds his hand and tells him he forgives him. The father dies in his hospital room in a very cold night.

The fourth person Eddie meets in heaven is Marguerite, his wife and the love of his life. He sees Marguerite in an Italian wedding then he sees other international weddings. This makes him remember their small and simple wedding that took place in a small Chinese restaurant. Marguerite tells him she has met her five people already and this has helped her come to a better understanding of life. Eddie remembers the watch she gave him on one of his birthdays that they used to celebrated in Ruby Pier. They both remember how they could not have a child of their own. They get busy with Marguerite brain tumor and forgot about the child. Eddie tells Marguerite what happened after her death. He tells her that new rides are added in Ruby Pier; dangerous rides that Eddie does not like. She takes him into a room decorated like the hall where they had their wedding. They dance a little then she disappears.

The fifth and last person Eddie meets in heaven is a little girl. He hears sounds of children playing by the river. One little Asian girl waves to him with both hands, and he walked to her. She introduces herself to him, Tala. She points to each piece of her clothes and names it in her language. She says that she and the kids are washing in the river like their mothers used to do to them. He makes her a dog from pipe cleaners in his pocket as he used to do to children in Ruby Pier. The girl tells Eddie that he burned her. She was the shadow in that hut that he burned when he escaped his prison in Philippine. Eddie gets very sad and cries aloud and asks her to forgive him. She gives him a stone and asked him to wash her in the river. As he rubs the stone against her body, her skin gets healed from the burns. He tells her that he has accomplished nothing in his life, she says he keeps children at Ruby Pier save and happy. Eddie asks Tala about the little girl in the cart incident. She says he pushed her away and saved her. Tala says that it was her own hands that he grabbed, not the little girl's. She takes him to heaven to keep him safe. Tala takes him trough all colors to the ocean. When he gets out of the water, he finds himself in Ruby Pier crowded with so many people; he sees Marguerite and realizes he is finally home.

After the summaries are given, the next step is to put similarities and differences between the novel and the book in a table such as table 11.

Novel	Both	Movie
-Minor details	- He is very considerate	- Minor details
- Never been to Mexico	- He fights for his older brother	- Never been to Miami
- Before his death he as dreaming of the beach with Marguerite and their song	- He rides the rides once a week	- before his death who was napping
- He makes animals to children from pipe cleaners	- At the accident, the cart wire gets loose and the cart falls.
- At the accident, Dominguez and Willie release the cart.	- He did not want to leave the burning hut because he thought he saw somebody inside.	- Blue Man crashes into a food stand
- Blue Man crashes into a parked truck.	- He sees Mickey attacking his mother from inside the apartment.
- He sees Mickey attacking his mother from a circle in the snow	- He took his father's job and gave up his dream job for his mother.	- His father dies at the hospital.
- His father dies at the hospital window	- He holds his father's hand at the diner and forgives him.
- He forgives his father at the diner.	- He died trying to save a little girl from the falling cart.	- Major details
- Major details	- Marguerite gives him a watch in his birthday.
- Eddie gambles in horse race.	- They forget about the adoption after Marguerite has a brain tumor.
- They forget about the adoption after Marguerite has a car accident.	

Table 11, Differences and similarities between novel and movie (the Five People You Meet in Heaven)

Based on the information in table 11, the thesis is structured as follows:

The story about The Five People You Meet in Heaven, along with similarities, is presented differently in the novel and the movie.

The next step is forming the outline for the essay.

Block Outline:

I. Introduction

a. General review

b. Thesis (The story about The Five People You Meet in Heaven, along with similarities, is presented differently in the novel and the movie).

II. Body

a. Topic sentence (Similarities).

i. Supporting detail # 1

1. Considerate and caring.

b. Topic sentence (Differences).

i. Supporting detail # 1 (Minor details).

1. Novel (minor details that only exist in the novel).

2. Movie (minor details that only exist in the movie).

ii. Supporting detail # 2 (major details).

1. Novel (major details that only exist in the novel)

2. Movie (major details that only exist in the movie).

III.   Conclusion

a. Thesis restatement.

b. General review.

Point-by-point Outline

I.   Introduction

a. General Review.

b. Thesis (The story about The Five People You Meet in Heaven, along with similarities, is presented differently in the novel and the movie).

II.   Body

a. Topic sentence (similarity # 1)

1. Supporting detail # 1 considerate and caring.

b. Topic sentence (difference # 1) (minor details)

1. Novel (minor details that only exist in the novel)

2. Movie (minor details that only exist in the movie)

c. Topic sentence (difference # 2) (major details)

1. Novel (major details that only exist in the novel)

2. Movie (major details that only exist in the movie)

III.   Conclusion

a. Thesis restatement.

b. General review

The Block Essay

The Five People You Meet in Heaven, a novel written by Mitch Albom is a very inspiring story about an old retired veteran named Eddie, who works as a maintenance man in an amusement park called Ruby Pier.

After he passes away, he comes to a better understanding about life. After he dies, he meets five people he has either known in his life or has some kind of indirect connection with them. The story about The Five People You Meet in Heaven, along with similarities, is presented differently in the novel and the movie.

The main similarity between the novel and the movie is the depiction of Eddie's character as considerate and caring. There are examples that show Eddie's care towards his family, his job, and other people. He fights for his older brother when he gets in trouble with other guys in the neighborhood. He gives up his dream job as an engineer and takes his father's job at Ruby Pier because he wants to take care of his mother after his father dies. Additionally, he rides in the Ruby Pier rides once a week to make sure everything functions perfectly. When he burns the huts in Philippine after he and his friends escape prison, he sees a figure of a person inside one burning hut and does not want to leave until he gets that person out of the fire. And finally he dies trying to save a little girl from a falling cart. Despite his constant announcement that he is useless and has achieved nothing in his life, he manages to give care and help to others.

In addition to these similarities, there are differences between the novel and movie that, though do not change the plot, still have significant effect on it. The first kind of difference is in minor details which do not have a significant effect on the events. One example is when Dominguez says in the novel that he is taking his wife to Mexico and Edie says he has never been there. In the movie, however, the place is changed to Miami. Likewise, minutes before the crash incident in Ruby Pier, Eddie is sitting on a chair with his eyes closed and dreams of Marguerite being with him at the beach. In the movie, Eddie is sitting on a chair and napping until the screaming shouts of the crowds wake him up. In a similar manner, while in the novel Dominguez and Willie are the ones who release the cart after getting everybody out of it, the movie shows the cart falls after the wire is cut off because of the pressure. One other minor difference is the accident that kills Blue Man. In the novel, Blue Man crashes his car into a parked truck and dies of a heart attack. The movie, on the other hand, shows Blue Man stepping out of the car after crashing it into a food stand and dies of a heart attack. When Eddie meets Ruby in the novel and she shows him how Mickey attacks his mother in her room, she shows him that through a circle she draws in the snow. This is differently presented in the movie in which Eddie sees the incident while being inside the apartment. The father's death is also different in the novel and the movie. The novel explains how the sick father dies at the hospital window, whereas the movie shows an empty hospital bed in one morning with the death being announced by the narrator. There is another difference about his last meeting with his father in heaven. While in the novel he tells his father at the diner that he forgives him with no physical contact, he touches his father's hand in the movie and holds it for some time. Although these details are minor, there are other major details that are more significant in both the novel and the movie. There are major details in the novel that are not mentioned in the movie and vice versa. For example, the novel talks about how Eddie gets addicted to horse race gambling and how Marguerite is upset with that. One day he calls her and tells her his horse has won, she yells at him on the phone because they want to save money and be more responsible in order to be able to adopt a child. This brings the second major detail that is given only in the novel. Marguerite decides to drive to the horse race to apologize to Eddie for yelling at him on his birthday. She has a car accident on her way and this costs them the adoption due to financial shortage and delay. On the other hand, the movie includes details that are not in the novel. For example, the movie shows Marguerite giving Eddie a watch as a present on one of his birthdays; Eddie is wearing the watch the time he dies. In other word, the watch represents their long lasting love that stays inside his heart after her death. The brain tumor Marguerite has is included in both the novel and the movie; however, in the movie, it is made the reason for not adopting a child, not the car accident as the novel tells.

The Five People You Meet in Heaven is a story that is made into a movie that carries similarities and differences with the novel. Although some of the differences are minor and do not change the events, other differences are significantly important because they present the story in different ways giving the reader and the viewer the chance to have multiple interpretations of the story.

The Point-by-point Essay

The Five People You Meet in Heaven, a novel written by Mitch Albom is a very inspiring story about an old retired veteran named Eddie, who works as a maintenance man in an amusement park called Ruby Pier. After he passes away, he comes to a better understanding about life. After he dies, he meets five people he has either known in his life or has some kind of indirect connection with them. The story about The Five People You Meet in Heaven, along with similarities, is presented differently in the novel and the movie.

The main similarity between the novel and the movie is the depiction of Eddie's character as considerate and caring. There are examples that show Eddie's care towards his family, his job, and other people. He fights for his older brother when he gets in trouble with other guys in the neighborhood. He gives up his dream job as an engineer and takes his father's job at Ruby Pier because he wants to take care of his mother after his father dies. Additionally, he rides in the Ruby Pier rides once a week to make sure everything functions perfectly. When he burns the huts in Philippine after he and his friends escape prison, he sees a figure of a person inside one burning hut and does not want to leave until he gets that person out of the fire. And finally he dies trying to save a little girl from a falling cart. Despite his constant announcement that he is useless and has achieved nothing in his life, he manages to give care and help to others.

In addition to these similarities, there are differences between the novel and movie that, though do not change the plot, still have significant effect on it. The first kind of difference is in minor details which do not have a significant effect in the event. One example is when Dominguez says in the novel that he is taking his wife to Mexico and Edie says he has never been there. In the movie, however, the place is changed to Miami. Likewise, minutes before the crash incident in Ruby Pier, Eddie is sitting on a chair with his eyes closed and dreams of Marguerite being with him at the beach. In the movie, Eddie is sitting on a chair and napping until the creaming shouts of the crowds wake him up. In a similar manner, while in the novel Dominguez and Willie are the ones who release the cart after getting everybody out of it, the movie shows the cart falls after the wire is cut off because of the pressure. One other minor difference is the accident that kills Blue Man. In the novel, Blue Man crashes his car into a parked truck and dies of a heart attack. The movie, on the other hand, shows Blue Man stepping out of the car after crashing it into a food stand and dies of a heart attack. When Eddie meets Ruby in the novel and she shows him how Mickey attacks his mother in her room, she shows him that through a circle she draws in the snow. This is differently presented in the movie in which Eddie sees the incident while being inside the apartment. The father's death is also different in the novel and the movie. The novel explains how the sick father dies at the hospital window, whereas the movie shows an empty hospital bed in one morning with the death being announced by the narrator. There is another difference about his last meeting with his father in heaven. While in the novel he tells his father at the diner that he forgives him with no physical contact, he touches his father's hand in the movie and holds it for some time. Although these details are minor, there are other major details that are more significant in both the novel and the movie.

There major details in the novel that are not mentioned in the movie and vice versa. For example, the novel talks about how Eddie gets addicted to horse race gambling and how Marguerite is upset with that. One day he calls her and tells her his horse has won, she yells at him on the phone because they want to save money and be more responsible in order to be able to adopt a child. This brings the second major detail that is given only in the novel. Marguerite decides to drive to the horse race to apologize to Eddie for yelling at him on his birthday. She has a car accident on her way and this costs them the adoption due to financial shortage and delay. On the other hand, the movie includes details that are not in the novel. For example, the movie shows Marguerite giving Eddie a watch as a present on one of his birthdays; Eddie is wearing the watch the time he dies. In other word, the watch represents their long lasting love that stays inside his heart after her death. The brain tumor Marguerite has is included in both the novel and the movie; however, in the movie, it is made the reason for not adopting a child, not the car accident as the novel tells.

The Five People You Meet in Heaven is a story that is made into a movie that carries similarities and differences with the novel. Although some of the differences are minor and do not change the events, other differences are significantly important because they present the story in different ways giving the reader and the viewer the chance to have multiple interpretations of the story.

Exercises

Exercise 1. Rewrite the following separate sentences into one full sentence by adding the appropriate transition words that indicate comparison or contrast.

1. In order to be accepted for the program, you need to get 25 or more in the math test. Another requirement is to have a score of 30 or above in the English placement test.
2. He already speaks three languages fluently. His little brother speaks these three languages as native tongue.
3. One other way to enter building D is from the rear door. The only way to enter building C is the front door.
4. The boy becomes very sad and cries whenever his mother leaves him with his babysitter. His young sister never stops crying until her mother comes back home.
5. She struggles with math every year. He has hard time studying chemistry.
6. She gets very happy every time she wins in chess game and celebrates the wining by inviting her friends for ice cream. She spends the weekend at home and refuses to see anyone after she loses the game.
7. The three students responsible for the lab spend the weekend in it to study for their physics final. They spend Friday evenings in the lab to work on their math assignments.
8. Jack has decided to major in philosophy. His friend Alex has not decided what to study yet.
9. I have a great passion in designing cards. My mother prefers pottery.
10. Some students suggest writing a paper to improve their grades. Other students want to retake the test.

Exercise 2. In the examples below, classify the items in each point into category A and category B in a Venn diagram or a table, then include as many similarities and differences between them as you possibly can.

1. Home schooling vs. going to school.
2. Living in a big city vs. living in a small city.
3. Living on campus vs. living off campus
4. TV commercials vs. radio commercials.
5. Calling vs. Texting.
6. Facebook vs. Instigram.
7. Travel by car vs. travel by plane.
8. Channel vs. Christian Dior.
9. Eating at home vs. eating in a restaurant.
10. Online classes vs. traditional classes.

Exercise 3. Choose at least three topics from exercise 2 and write a block outline and a point-by-point outline for each one of them. After that, use the information you have in the outlines to write compare and contrast essays for these topics.

Exercise 4. Table 12 contains information about the differences and similarities between Eukaryotic and Prokaryotic cells which constitute human physiology. Eukaryotic cells are organisms with cell nucleus enclosed inside membranes among other organelles. On the other hand, Prokaryotic cells are unicellular organisms which do not have cell nucleus or other organelles enclosed inside the membranes.

Based on the information provided in table12, write a compare and contrast essay that explains the similarities and differences between Eukaryotic and Prokaryotic cells.

Eukaryotic Cells	Both	Prokaryotic Cells
- Size: 10-100um. - Includes specialized organelles, e.g. endoplasmic reticulum. - There linear DNA is bound into chromosomes by packaging proteins known as histones. - Can be single-celled or multi-celled. - Sexual reproduction. - Cell division: mitosis then cytokinesis.	- Both are cells. - Genetic materials: both cells contain plasma membrane, DNA, cytoplasm and ribosomes. - Chemical structure: consist of carbohydrates nucleic acid, vitamins, proteins, minerals, and fats. - Both cells regulate nutrient flows into the cellules and waste matter outside of them.	- Size: 1-10um. - Includes bacteria and archaea. - Lack membrane-bound nucleus and organelle. - Have circular DNA inside the membrane. - contains no histones nor chromosomes. - Only single-celled (unicellular). - Asexual reproduction (cells reproduces clones of themselves). - Cell division; binary fission.

Table 12, some differences and similarities between Eukaryotic and Prokaryotic cells

Exercise 5. Below is information about two individuals: individual A is Abdulmonji, and individual B is Ramadan. Read the information about each one of them and fill it in a Venn diagram or a table that shows similarities and difference between them. Then use the information to write a block or a point-by point outline. After that, write a block essay or a point-by-point compare and contrast essay that discusses points of similarities and differences between the two gentlemen.

A. Abdulmonji   B. Ramadan

A.   Renovation and adventure give meaning to life and make it worth living. My name is Abdulmonji, I have a high school diploma, and I am married with two sons. I work at Misrata International Airport. I also manage a Coffee Import and Processing Company, and I am an administrative in a contracting company in addition to other businesses. I like diving and fishing and I love going in wild trips for hunting, camping, and travelling to exotic places with friends. I have a special passion for flying; it feels good and relaxing to fly and watch the world from above. Everything looks small from a plane, including problems, and that is one of the reasons I feel comfortable when flying. It is my desire to own a private jet one day. I also dream of founding a private Aviation Academy in Misrata that includes professional trainers in this field.

B.   For Ramadan, life means devotion and dedication. He is the director of the Civil Society Commission in Misrata. He has a bachelor's degree in Chemistry and is a hard-working father of five children. In addition to his current job, he is a businessman, and a free-lance writer in a number of local newspapers in Misrata. He has experience in other different jobs in the past. He is a former member in the Media Committee in Misrata and used to be a presenter in one of Misrata local radio station programs. Additionally, he is among the pioneers who have launched the first TV channel in Misrata, and he is the script writer of the movie *The Way to Wow* in 2013. Moreover, he gave a number of courses and workshops in journalism and business management. In addition to his jobs, Ramadan has a number of hobbies that he enjoys such as reading, sketching, photography, jewelry design, gardening, swimming, fishing and travelling among others. Although he has not actually worked within the field of his specialty; i.e. chemistry, Ramadan likes to keep his schedule busy because he enjoys participating in many activities and is determined to devote himself to have a successful loving family and contribute to the development of his community.

Exercise 6. The following are summaries of a movie and a novel. Read the summaries carefully, then write a compare and contrast essay about the two main characters in the two stories (Norman in *Psycho* and Emily in *A Rose for Emily*) by following the steps explained in this chapter, e.g. Venn diagram table, block outline, and point-by-point outline.

- *Psycho* (1960): a movie directed by Alfred Hitchcock
- *A Rose for Emily* (1930): a novel written by William Faulkner.

Psycho (1960)

The movie tells the story of Marion, a secretary in a real estate office in Phoenix, Arizona who is no longer interested in her job because of the way her boss treats her. Also, she has a secret romantic relationship with a man called Sam who tells her he is in need for money to pay for his debts. Marion is trusted by her employer to deposit an amount of $40,000 in the bank; but instead, she takes the money and decides to leave her job and the city and go to California where her boyfriend lives. She acts very suspiciously as she drives out of the city, especially when the police officer sees her sleeping inside her car on her way to California. To be more cautious, she decides to buy a new car, but she still acts uncomfortably because the police officer follows her to the auto agent. She buys a new car and hits the road again.

As it gets darker, it starts to rain heavily. Marion cannot continue driving, so she checks in a small isolated motel run by a young man named Norman. The young guy acts nicely and invites Marion to a simple dinner in the motel's kitchen. When Marion gets in the motel room, she hears the voices of Norman and his mother arguing over her spending the night in the motel. While having dinner, Norman tells Marion that his mother has mental issues and he refuses to send her to an institution that he calls 'Mad House'. When Marion goes back to her room, she decides to take a shower, and Norman watches her secretly from a peephole on the wall in his office. While Marion is taking a shower, a woman with a butcher knife appears out of sudden and stabs Marion to death. After Norman learns about what happens, he rushes to the motel room and sees Marion dead in the shower. He puts Marion's body, along with her belongings, inside the trunk of her car, and then he goes back to the room where the murder takes place and cleans up the miss. After that, he drives Marion's car into a swamp nearby and watches it sink.

After the death of Marion, her sister Lila starts the search for her. She asks Sam if he knows anything about Marion's sudden disappearance and he confirms that he has no idea. Additionally, a private investigator named Abrogast gets involved in the case and stays in touch with Lila and Sam. The investigator manages to track Marion to the small motel where she is murdered. He asks Norman some questions then he requests to interrogate Norman's mother, but Norman refuses and the investigator leaves the motel.

Mr. Abrogast contacts Lila and talks to her about his suspicions towards Norman and his desire to go back to the motel and interrogate Norman another time. The investigator goes back to the motel and finds no one, so he decides to check the house next door where Norman and his mother live. He opens the door and takes a look inside. As the investigator goes up the stairs, Norman's mother attacks him with a knife and stabs him to death.

As Lila and Sam wait for Abrogast to show up, Lila decides to go to the motel and check the situation herself, but Sam suggests he goes instead. Sam goes to the motel and calls out for Abrogast but no one answers. However, Sam notices the figure of an old woman inside the house who seems like she can hear him but never replies. As a result, he goes back to Lila and the two of them decide to contact the local Deputy Sheriff Chambers. The Sherriff calls the motels and asks about Mr. Abrogast. Norman confirms that the investigator has come to the motel and asked Norman some questions about Marion and then left. Moreover, the Sherriff informs Lila that Norman's mother has passed away ten years ago after poisoning her lover and herself. This confuses Lila and Sam who remember Mr. Abrogast telling them that Norman has refused to let him investigate his mother. Norman, being worried from the occasional visits of those people to his motel, appears taking his mother by force from her room and putting her inside a fruit cellar as an attempt to hide her from people.

Lila and Sam go to the motel as a couple looking for a room to spend the night in. At the hotel, Sam distracts Norman while Lila goes out to look for Norman's mother in order to talk to her. Norman gets suspicious and clubs Sam on the head with a vase and goes after Lila. Lila takes a look inside the house and attempts to leave it, but she sees Norman coming so she decides to hide inside the fruit cellar. Inside the room, Lila sees the back of a figure of an old man sitting on the chair. Lila turns the chair around and is shocked to see a skeleton in a dress and a wig. Lila gives a loud scream as Norman rushes into the room holding a knife and wearing a dress and a wig that look like the ones on the skeleton. Norman tries to attack Lila but he is stopped by Sam. After that, the police arrives.

Investigation shows that Norman is mentally unstable and he is taken over by his mother's character and she has control over him. Moreover, after Norman killed his mother and her lover out of jealousy, he stole her corpse and kept it inside the house. Ever since, he has conversations with his mother and assumes she has similar jealousy over his love life and accordingly becomes wild whenever a woman is involved in his life. At the end, the movie ends with a scene of Norman in the police station with the mother's personality dominating him.

A Rose for Emily (1930)

Emily Grierson is born into a rich high class Southern aristocratic family. Ever since she was a child, she has been isolated from the rest of the world by her overprotective father. Emily is raised as a traditional lady of old south who cannot accept change and new ideas. Her father keeps rejecting men who propose to her, depriving her from having a new life. Emily's aunt, who is mentally unstable, lives with them in the house.

After the death of her father, the thirty-year-old Emily confirms to ladies who come to offer their condolences that her father is not dead, and she lives in this denial for three whole days. Town leaders go to Emily and ask to bury her father. She finally accepts her father's death as a reality and turns his body over for burial. This incident causes a mental break down for Emily and leaves her deeply sad and sick and rarely leaves the house.

The next summer, construction workers come to town to pave the town's sidewalks. Among the workers is a young man from the North called Homer Barron. Emily meets Homer and she starts to go out with him paying no attention to the people's gossip about her that she is scandalizing the legacy of her family by getting involved with a man of a lower status and a different regional background. The word spreads in the town that Emily is likely to marry Homer; however, Homer expresses that he is not the marrying type and he likes to spend more time with other guys in the club.

As the gossip continues and the risk of compromising Emily's reputation increases, she decides to go to the local drug store and buy arsenic. People think that she plans to poison herself after Homer's announcement of his intention to stay unmarried. People in town write to Emily's relatives to come to town and watch over her. Homer leaves the town for a period of time before he returns again.

A rumor spreads in town that Emily and Homer are getting married because Emily buys men's toilet set in silver with the letters H and B engraved on each piece. One day at sun set, Homer is seen coming into Emily's house but never seen again after that. Days pass and Emily never leaves the house.

An awful smell spreads out of Emily's house and the neighbors complain. But nobody desires to confront Emily because she is well-known for being unresponsive to requests as she refuses to pay her taxes and tell the druggist the reason why she buys arsenic. As a result, some town people sneak to Emily's house in the middle of the night and sprinkle lime all around it in an attempt to reduce the ghastly smell that has been bothering everybody.

After spending the rest of her life alone inside the house, Emily dies at the age of seventy-four. The whole town goes to see her and her relatives from Alabama return to attend the funeral. It is noticed that there is a locked room in the house. People open it and find bridal stuff and silver toiletry set inside. They also find a skeleton on the bed that is dressed in men's clothes. On the other pillow next to the skeleton, they find an indentation that indicates somebody has been sleeping next to the decomposed body, and they find a long strand of iron gray hair on the pillow.

Exercise 7. The following are summaries of a novel and the movie based on the novel. Read the summaries carefully, then write a compare and contrast essay about the similarities and differences of events between the novel and the movie.

- *Sarah Plain and Tall* (1985): a novel written by Patricia MacLachlan.
- *Sarah Plain and Tall* (1991): a movie directed by Glen Jordan.

Summary of *Sarah Plain and Tall,* the story.

The novel events take place in the late nineteenth century. The story is about a widower named Jacob Witting who has lost his wife and has to take care of their two children, Anna and Caleb in addition to farming. While Anna remembers how her mother and her father used to sing to her, Caleb has no memories of his mother because she passed away giving birth to him. Anna takes charge of household chores despite her young age and she makes food to her father and brother. The father has stopped singing after his wife's death and decided to do his best to provide care to his children. Jacob is having a hard time looking after the kids and the farm. Therefore, he places an advertisement in a newspaper seeking a wife; a mail-order bride service which is previously done by their neighbors to get a wife from Tennessee. A single lady from Maine named Sarah Wheaton sees the advertisement, responds to it and decides to travel to them. Sarah tells Jacob's family that she has a cat named Seal, and Anna wants to know if Sarah can sing. The kids exchange letters with Sarah who tells them that she loves the sea. The kids are worried that Sarah may not like getting away from the sea and live in a farm. Sarah decides to stay in the farm temporarily for one month to make a decision about this marriage. She informs the Witting family that she will travel by train and that she is a tall and plain lady with a yellow bonnet.

On Sarah's arrival day, Jacob takes the wagon and rides a pretty long distance to the train station to pick her up. Anna and Caleb prepare themselves and the house to welcome Sarah. Caleb keeps asking his sister if Sarah will like them and bring the sea with her. The kids hear the dog barking and Caleb sees a yellow bonnet; they know that Sarah has arrived. Sarah brings a seashell for Caleb and a sea stone for Anna who wants Sarah to like their life in the farm so she does not leave them. Although Sarah misses the sea and her seashell collection, she manages to learn farm work with the help of Caleb who welcomes her more openly and willingly than his sister.

The dogs love Sarah and Seal starts to act comfortably. Sarah teaches Caleb how to put the seashell to his ear to hear the sound of the ocean. Caleb, unlike his father and his sister who act very shyly, talks to Sarah all day. Sarah teaches the children how to dry flowers by hanging them down from the ceiling. Caleb loves the flowers and makes up a song about them that makes everybody laugh as they sit at the table for dinner that Sarah has made. Also, Sarah gives Caleb a haircut and scatters the hair on the ground so that the birds use it to build their nests, and she combs Anna's hairs in a nice way that Anna likes. They notice that Sarah says *Ayuh* instead of *Yes* because that is how people in Maine respond; Caleb starts using *Ayuh* too. Sarah sings with the children at the porch and asks Caleb to show her the sheep because she has never seen them before.

Sarah likes the sheep and gives them her aunt's names; but she gets upset when she sees one of the lambs dead. Jacob helps her bury it. Sarah tells the children that she misses the sea and the sand dunes. Jacob shows her the dunes they have in the farm which they call hey stacks and tells Sarah and the kids to throw themselves into them. That night, Sarah writes to her family in Maine and tells them about the dunes.

Caleb tells Sarah that it snows in winter and the children go to school regardless of the inclement weather in the wagon. Sarah wants to swim but there is no sea in the farm, so she decides to use the cow pond to teach the kids how to swim and play in the water. After that, they lay down in the field to dry up, and the kids feel positive that Sarah is staying.

One day, Sarah joins the kids on the porch to watch Jacob and their neighbor plow the cornfield. Maggie the neighbor, who has married her husband through newspaper advertisement, comes to visit Sarah with her two daughters. The two ladies talk about how they both miss where they come from; Anna listens to their conversation. Before leaving, Maggie gives Sarah some plants to grow in the garden and tells Sarah to come visit sometime. Sarah says she does not know how to drives a wagon. Maggie also gives Sarah some chicken; but Sarah tells the kids that they will keep the chicken and give them names instead of eating them. That day, Jacob comes home with roses for Sarah.

Sarah wants to learn how to drive the wagon and how to ride the horse named Jack. Jacob agrees to teach her to drive the wagon but tells her that Jack is a sly horse for a beginner like her. However, Jacob agrees to let her ride Jack upon her insistence but after he fixes the roof. She offers her help in fixing the roof because she has done that before. Anna learns about Sarah's desire to go to the town in the wagon by herself; Anna is worried that Sarah may be thinking of leaving them. Suddenly, a storm comes and Jacob tells Sarah and the children to get all the animals inside the barn and stay with them. Sarah has to leave the barn to bring the chicken inside and Jacob freaks out and follows her. They manage to go back to the barn safely and they wait for the storm to stop. While waiting, Sarah and Jacob get closer and the children feel happy. They spend the night in the barn to stay safe from the storm. The next morning they leave the barn and see the whole place covered in hail.

After the storm, the field is damaged but the roof holds up due to the good work of Jacob and Sarah. Jacob starts teaching Sarah how to drive a wagon; the thing that makes Caleb suspicious that Sarah may leave them. He even cries when he sees how fast she is learning. One morning, Sarah wakes up early and starts getting ready to drive the wagon to the town. Jacob tells her to be back before dark and the three of them watch her leaving. Caleb thinks that Sarah has left to Maine because of him being loud and pesky. Anna comforts him by saying that Sarah would let them know if she has an intention to go back to Maine. When the children ask their father about Sarah, he says he has no idea where she is going and that she is an independent lady who can do things her own way. Anna knows for sure that Sarah is coming back because she has left her cat Seal with them; so instead of preparing the table for three, she prepares it for four.

When the three of them hear the dogs barking, they know Sarah is back. They hurry outside and Caleb hugs her and says with his eyes filled with tears that he thought she has left to Maine because she misses the sea. Sarah tells them that she has missed them too and that she went to the town to buy coloring pencils in the colors of blue, grey, and green because they are the colors of the sea. Sarah decides to stay and have a loving life with them. They prepare for the wedding and they have a drawing of the sea hanging on one of the house walls.

Summary of *Sarah Plain and Tall,* the movie.

The movie starts with a scene of the father Jacob working in the farm and his son Caleb asking Anna bout their mother's songs and blaming himself for her death. The father tells his children that he has placed an advertisement in the newspaper for a wife. A single lady from Maine named Sarah Wheaton responds to the advertisement and writes back to Jacob's family. Sarah tells them that she lives by the sea and although she loves it, she is willing to travel. The children exchange letters with Sarah to get to know her and Caleb wants to know if Sarah sings. Sarah tells them that she has a cat named Seal and that her favorite colors are blue, gray and green because they are the colors of the sea in different kinds of weather. Sarah decides to travel to them because she wants to have her chance to have her own life.

The Witting neighbor, Maggie, wants to know if Anna is comfortable with the idea of a new mother. Anna tells Maggie that she is not sure if Sarah wants to stay with them because she loves the sea. Sarah tells them she is coming for a month to see if she can make a change, and she will be wearing a yellow bonnet.

Jacobs goes to the train station to pick Sarah up. Anna is scared she might forget her mother when Sarah arrives. When Sarah gets out of the train, she does not find Jacob, so she decides to buy a ticket back to Maine. After buying the ticket she sees Jacob standing by her. He takes her luggage on the wagon and takes her to his house. Anna keeps herself busy in sewing while Caleb asks her one question after the other: is my face clean? What if she does not like our house? Will she be nice like Maggie? How far away is Maine? Will she like us? Anna answers patiently.

The way back from the station is long enough to start a conversation between Sarah and Jacob. He tells her how his wife died six years ago and he expresses his hope that she does not mind the imperfection of the house. Caleb shouts that he sees a yellow bonnet; Sarah has arrived. Sarah gives Caleb a big seashell and she gives a sea stone to Anna, she also shows them her cat. The first question Caleb asks Sarah is if she can sing and she says she does.

When she wakes up in the morning, Sarah sees the dog next to her bed; she takes the cat outside and takes a look around the untidy house. She goes outside the house and finds Jacob and his children already up and working in the barn. Jacob invites Sarah to see the animals but she suggests walking first. She insures to him that she is used to work and would love to help in the farm. The children, who are watching from the barn, have doubts that Sarah may not like farm life. Sarah shows her seashell collection to Caleb and teaches him to hold them to his ear to hear the sea. In addition, Sarah teaches Caleb how to dance while Jacob is watching, and he helps her collecting flowers to hang them on the ceiling and dry them for winter. Jacob is so excited that Sarah is already thinking of winter because this means there is a chance for her to stay with them longer. Caleb uses flower names to make a song while Sarah prepares dinner. They notice that Sarah says *Ayuh* instead of *Yes* because that is how people in Maine respond; Caleb starts using *Ayuh* too. Sarah sings with the children at the porch as she sews; then Jacob joins them. Sarah asks Caleb to show her the sheep because she wants to touch them.

Sarah starts walking at night, and Jacob comes to her and talks about how he wants this to work, and she agrees with him. The next morning, she gives Caleb a haircut at the porch while talking to him about her family. Then she spreads his hair on the farm ground for the birds to build nests. Caleb gets happy because that means Sarah will stay with them. Sarah, who notices how Anna is quite and lonely, asks Anna's if she can make her hair while talking about how she had lost her mother too when she was ten. That night, Sarah hears Anna crying in her sleep and hurries to comfort her. Jacob tells Sarah that Anna has been having these nightmares ever since her mother died. Sarah tells Jacob that he needs to accept his wife's death but he tells her not to interfere in that matter and that he runs the household on his own way.

The next day, the four of them go to a picnic and Sarah notices that everybody stares at her. Jacob tells her that he tells people she is an old family friend. They meet Mathew and his wife Maggie who assures to Sarah that town people are very nice. They also meet a lady named Mavens who, as Anna states, likes Jacob and invites him to dinner sometimes. When Caleb asks Sarah to dance with him, a man comes and motions to Caleb to go away so he can dance with Sarah instead. Feeling jealous, Jacob goes to Sarah and asks for a dance with her and she agrees. The children watch the dancing couple joyfully.

Sarah continues learning farm job and tells Jacob she wants to learn how to ride a wagon and a horse. Jacob tells Sarah that he knew his wife as children and that he loved her; Sarah tells him he still does. Sarah and the children give the sheep different names, and then she suggests that they go swimming in the pond. She teaches them how to swim and play in the water. When Jacob comes, he finds the three of them lay on the grass to dry up. Anna tells him that she has a nice dream and Sarah is happy. In the evening, the kids join Sarah in her drawing and she tells them she misses the dunes. Jacob takes them to the hay stack to jump over it. It is a bonding moment between Sarah and Jacob as the kids jump over the hay stack.

The next morning, Mathew and his wife Maggie visit the Wittings. Maggie gives Sarah some chicken to make food, but Anna insists that chicken are not to be eaten. Maggie also brings some flowers to Sarah to plant them in the garden, and then the two ladies sit at the porch and exchange experience of missing where they come from. Sarah tells Maggie that Jacob does not want to let go of his wife's memory. Sarah tells Jacob that she has her own small garden now. Sarah also tells Maggie that she wants to learn how to ride a wagon; both Maggie and Anna offer to teach her.

One day, Sarah goes with Jacob and the kids to the town to do some shopping. Sarah buys home-made canned peaches despite Anna's notice that they are not very good. On their way home, Anna asks if they are going to stop to visit her mother's grave but Jacob disagrees regardless of Sarah's request to do so. Sarah finds a small lamb dead and she gets so sad because she becomes attached to the sheep.

Sarah offers to help Jacob in fixing the house roof while the children put the animals inside the barn because of the coming storm. Sarah insists to find her cat Seal first and Jacob goes out with her to find the cat. Sarah freaks out and says she should not have come here in front of Anna who gets upset. While they all go inside the barn and wait for the storm to stop, they hear the hail hitting the roof of the barn. The next morning, they leave the barn and Anna is sad to see the flowers in Sarah's little garden dead because of the storm. Jacob tells Sarah they need to sell the sheep to cover the storm damage. Sarah offers her money but Jacob refuses sharply; Sarah tells him he shuts everyone out because he still loves his wife. Jacob tells her that he and the children like her. Mathew and his wife come to help Jacob and Sarah repair the damage caused by the storm. Sarah finds Seal on the roof and gets so happy for his safety; this makes Anna think that Sarah may be leaving them. Anna starts teaching Sarah how to ride a wagon, the two of them go to visit Anna's mother's grave. Anna asks Sarah if she is leaving and Sarah tells her that Jacob wants a woman she cannot be. Anna begs Sarah to try for the sake of Caleb. Matthew comes to tell them that Maggie is giving birth to her baby. Sarah rushes to Maggie to help her. Jacob hears the cries and rushes outside. Sarah follows him to the barn and he tells her that his wife was too young when Anna was born. The doctor told them not to have another child but he needed a boy so she got pregnant again but died giving birth to Caleb.

The next morning, Sarah gets dressed and rides the wagon to the town. Jacob tells her to be back before the dark. Jacob and the kids watch her leave sadly. Caleb says that Sarah is definitely leaving but Anna tells him she is not leaving because she has left her cat with them. The kids ask their father why Sarah has left, and he says she does things on her way. Anna does not find the train ticket in Sarah's drawer and tells her father that Sarah is gone to Maine. Jacob takes his horse and rushes to the train station. He sees the train leaving so he thinks he is late. But then he sees Sarah and she tells him that she has returned her ticket and got her money back because she wants to help repairing the storm damage. The children see the wagon with their father and Sarah on it and Caleb gives Sarah a big hug. She tells them that although she misses home, she will miss them more if she leaves. Sarah hands them coloring pencils with the colors of the sea and the movie ends in a beautiful wedding for Sarah and Jacob.

CPSIA information can be obtained
at www.ICGtesting.com
Printed in the USA
LVHW011649260623
750800LV00002B/31